An Unexpected Journey

A Physician's Life in the Shadow of Polio

Lauro S. Halstead, M.D.

For

Jessica

&

Larissa, Christina and Alexander

Acknowledgments

I am grateful to Pamela Toutant, Victoria Kohl
and Kathleen Wheaton for their professional
guidance and many helpful insights in writing
this memoir.

Author's Note

The events I relate here are real. Some names,
dates and locations have been altered to main-
tain confidentiality and enhance the narrative
flow.

Contents

Preface

In the summer of 1954 after my freshman year at college, I became deathly ill with polio while hitchhiking in Europe. When my breathing gave out, my 18-year-old paralyzed body was placed in a wooden mechanical respirator in a hospital in Madrid, Spain.

Even though I wasn't Catholic, because of the touch-and-go nature of my illness, I was offered last rites by the hospital priest which prompted me to gasp, "Go to hell!"

Refusing that priest's offer was a turning point. I remember thinking, *No, God damn it! I'm not ready to die.* The respirator pumped fresh air into my lungs and fresh thoughts into my brain, *I'm young. My life is just beginning. There's so many things I want to do.*

I wasn't thinking of becoming a physician—or anything else—in that moment, but I was excited about what adventures might lie ahead. Now, decades later, I have decided to look back at some of those adventures in an effort to understand the choices I made and the person I became. Through the slow, demanding process of writing, I hoped to gain greater insight into how I went from one stepping stone to another—rising from a near-death experience like the mythical phoenix and gradually, through a series of hits and misses, carving out a life that had meaning and joy.

Many events and people have contributed to this unexpected journey, a journey that has seldom followed a straight and narrow path as I struggled with issues of love and career, friendships and illness.

After I left the hospital in Madrid, I was flown back to the States, where I spent five months in a rehabilitation facility. Slowly, my breathing stabilized, the strength in my left arm improved and my legs were strong enough to walk without braces. However, the muscles in my right arm and shoulder never came back to life and remained permanently paralyzed. When I returned to college, I took up the task of living as best I could with only one good arm.

In contrast to many other polio survivors, my disability was extremely mild unless there was an activity that required two arms or two hands. Then I was very impaired which led me to choose activities I could do with one hand. As mild as my polio disability was, however, it has been a constant companion that has colored every aspect of my life: relationships, work, career, even making love. In darkness and light, polio has been an ever present shadow.

Any memoir is purposefully selective and as this book is *not* an autobiography, I have chosen to leave out most of my early life as well as many details of my personal relationships dealing with my current wife, Jessica, my former wife, Kris, and my three grown children. Suffice it to say that my family has been an integral part of my growth and maturation as well as the source of endless love and inspiration in the experiences described in the following pages.

This memoir is divided into 14 chapters and a Prologue and Afterword which serve as bookends to my life story. The Prologue, you might say, looks forward. It introduces the reader to my family and an old farm house in southern Vermont called "Storm Acres" that was originally used for vacations and later became a year around home when my parents retired. For me, because of the timeless beauty of the landscape and the loving presence of my parents, it was a magical refuge for both body and spirit throughout the many years of my life.

The Afterword, by contrast, is more of a glance backward. It attempts to sum up some of the themes I've touched on in the previous chapters as well as to answer questions people often ask about my experience with disability and aging.

One of the pleasures of writing this book is

the opportunity it gives me to dedicate this memoir to my loving wife, Jessica—who has added joy to my life along with comfort, support and nurturing beyond measure for almost a quarter century—and to my three precious children: Larissa, Christina and Alexander.

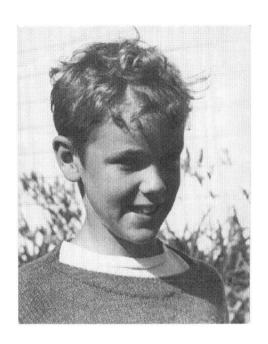

Me at age 5

Prologue:
Storm Acres

My parents, Helen Honsinger Halstead and Gordon Brinckerhoff Halstead, weren't planning on spending the summer of 1938 vacationing in southern Vermont. On the contrary, that part of Vermont was simply the bridge one had to cross driving from New York City to the "Northeast Kingdom", a rugged corner of the state just below the Canadian border. In those days, Vermont was celebrated for its rural, undeveloped landscape of low-lying mountains, wooden covered bridges and rocky terrain with more cows than people. Thus, it wasn't surprising that it took a sudden, summer downpour and muddy, one-lane roads to stop my parents and their three small children in their tracks in the small village of Peru, Vermont with its population of less than 200 inhabitants that year.

As I was born in 1936, I was the youngest of the travelers that summer and have no memory of any events. But the others in the car did, including my paternal grandmother, Rita Storm Halstead, and my brother, Scott Barker Halstead, who was eight, and my sister, Welthy Honsinger Halstead, who was five. Our car was miles from the Canadian border and any respectable civilization. Yet, stopping for the night in Peru turned out to be serendipity at its best.

When the sun dried the golden fields and the verdant mountains floated into view, my parents realized they were "stuck" in paradise. Over the course of several weeks, but with the impulsiveness of youth, they'd spent their life savings on a house more suitable to a farmer than to an urban high school teacher, but that house changed and enriched my family's life forever afterwards. The place had no electricity, telephone, or regular running water, and it was a 200-mile commute back to White Plains, a suburb of New York City. However, over the years, many others have discovered what my parents seemed to understand from the beginning: Vermont is a destination of enchantment and endless allure.

*****

For my parents, buying a summer house in rural Vermont in the middle of the Depression was the result of a series of fortuitous decisions—an inexplicable stroke of luck that endured, beyond any reasonable reckoning, until their deaths.

What they purchased that summer was much more than a stately old farmhouse nestled in the Green Mountains and surrounded by sixty-five acres of meadows, streams and woodlands: it was a retreat into yesterday and a refuge from tomorrow; it was a place that created lifelong memories for all of us. It was a paradise called Storm Acres.

A paradise in Vermont? Perhaps it was the remote isolation in a bucolic setting; perhaps it was the sensation of having traveled back a century or two when it was a working farm and life was simple but hard; perhaps it was the miraculous story of how it came into our family and then became a sacred place of self-renewal, where we stood tall in the cool mountain air. Maybe it was the smell of birch logs burning in the library fireplace; maybe the taste of wild red raspberries picked in a nearby field; or simply the sound of mice nestling in the bedroom walls. It was all of this and more, but especially, it was the presence of my parents who treated each new visitor like a royal guest in their mountain kingdom.

"This home has beautiful, invisible arms that reach out to give you a hug." my mother used to say to newcomers as she greeted them with an embrace. With its thick, hand-hewn ceiling beams and uneven floorboards, the house had an inviting charm that seemed to whisper *Welcome* whenever one stepped inside.

The name of the place, Storm Acres, came from the fact that a summer storm had played a role in my parents finding this house. Coincidentally, "Storm" was my paternal grandmother's maiden name. Initially, it was a rustic vacation home, but eventually, after installing modern conveniences such as electricity and a telephone, my parents used it as a fulltime residence during their retirement. Although I never lived there for more than a summer, for all the seasons of my life, through good times and bad, it was a still point for me and many others, around which our lives and destinies played out.

It was at Storm Acres that my mother and father came into their own as individuals and as a couple—a kind of power couple, without money—high up in the mountains. They moved there in 1968, and for more than three decades enjoyed vibrant health, mutual esteem and an equilibrium that allowed them to share their home and enthusiasm for life with everyone they encountered. They were remarkable people, who reflected the great American values of the 20th century. Among their many legacies, I inherited their passion for liberal politics and social justice as well as their humanists' sensibility about our place in the universe. Friends of mine who experienced their presence for even a few hours left in awe. Being with my parents at Storm Acres was ever magic.

Winter, 1948

In summer, it was a five to six-hour drive to Storm Acres from White Plains, where I grew up. During summer vacations, we might stay for two or three months. In the fall or winter, however, our visits were limited to long weekends. Trips in winter were a special treat, as several ski resorts were developed on nearby mountains after the war. There was one memorable ski trip with my father in 1948 when I was 12 years old and a good enough skier to make coming down the mountain fun.

"Make sure your bag is packed," my mother said that Friday afternoon when I got home from school. "Your father should be home shortly and he won't want to waste any time before hitting the road." There were going to be four of us sharing this ski weekend. Dad was bringing a friend from work and I had invited a friend from school.

I noticed it was snowing and called excitedly to my mother to look out the window. The forecast had predicted six to eight inches of new snow on the ski slopes by Saturday morning. Our weekend in the mountains promised to be a daring adventure.

"Maybe the storm will be bigger than anyone thought," I said, trying to conceal my excitement. "And we'll get snowed in at the house and I'll have to miss school on Monday." This was every schoolboy's dream.

The snowstorm did turn out to be bigger than predicted, and because the driveway up to Storm Acres was buried under two feet of snow, we had to ski over a mile to get to the house. We arrived close to midnight, exhausted, cold and hungry. The house had no electricity or central heating, so we spread our sleeping bags in front of the library fireplace. And there was no running water, so in the morning, we melted snow for making coffee and brushing our teeth. Drifts of snow stood as high as sixteen feet around the house, so getting back and forth to the ski slopes or the local store took most of the day and all of our energy. But who cared? It was the adventure of a lifetime.

Spring, 1970

There were other times when I traveled to Storm Acres under less sanguine circumstances: to heal a physical wound after surgery or to ease a broken heart. In early June 1970, I drove up to the house to tell my parents that my unhappy marriage to Joscelind four years earlier was ending in divorce. Fortunately, she and I had no children, but I still worried about what my parents would say. This was the first divorce in our family, a precedent I didn't like to be setting. *Will they think I'm a quitter or that I make bad decisions?* The self-doubts grew louder and more insistent the closer I got to my destination.

"I'm afraid I have bad news," I said to my parents when we were finally settled on the large, unscreened side porch. They looked at me with nervous, unsure smiles. A mild breeze drifted across the porch, carrying the fragrance of the purple lilacs and phlox flowering in the nearby meadow. "It's about my marriage," I finally blurted out, as though confessing a major crime. I sucked in a breath of air. And held it.

"Joscelind and I have been seeing a marriage counselor. We both agree. It's over and we're going to get a divorce."

My parents looked at me, not with surprise, but with admiration.

My mother spoke first. "You know, we're not at all surprised. And I wouldn't say this is bad news. As far as I'm concerned, it's good news. Whatever you decide to do, we'll support you a hundred percent." It was classic Helen: quick, pragmatic, decisive, and loving.

I looked over at my father. He had tears in his eyes. "I'm proud of you," he managed to say, his voice breaking. He paused to take out a handkerchief and wipe his eyes. "Yes, I'd say this is wonderful news. But..." He was searching for just the right words. Then, "It can't be easy and I admire your courage."

It was an unusual display for a man who

wasn't comfortable expressing emotion. Both of my parents had let me know of their abiding love and support. Suddenly, the summer air felt cooler and sweeter. What a joyous place to call home! I felt twice blessed to be within the loving bosom of my family while nestled in the tender heart of the surrounding mountains.

Summer, 1972

One afternoon in the late summer of 1972, I drove up to Storm Acres with Edward, an old friend from medical school. "Wait until you see it," I said as my own excitement mounted. Each return trip up into the mountains was a fresh adventure. We had just turned onto a narrow secondary road that led through a thick grove of birch and pines. I opened the windows so we could enjoy the rich forest aroma. "You're going to love it. It's the most peaceful place on earth and, at night, the stars are so bright you can read a book."

The car wound along a rutted dirt road for more than a mile and then, all at once, we left the shadows of the woods and burst into an open clearing flooded with sunlight.

I felt I was seeing Storm Acres for the first time through my friend's eyes. The broad white clapboards gave it a distinctly New England feel, enhanced by the way the house was set back at an angle from the road on a gentle slope of lawn. Portions of the house had been built in the early 19th century, and it retained a stately, noble character. Long green meadows stretched away from the house, and from the front porch, one could look out over a lush valley and low-lying mountains that rolled off slowly in the distance.

"Welcome," I whispered to Edward as we entered the front door. "This is paradise."

"We've been waiting for you," my mother said as she reached out to give him a hug. "Do you feel it? Can you feel how the house puts its arms around you?"

My friend looked around at the odd mixture of furniture that included a grandfather clock in one corner and a Franklin wood-burning stove toward the middle of the room and next to it a Gandhi spinning wheel. "Of course I do," he said smiling. "It feels absolutely marvelous."

Storm Acres on a summer day

Dining with Mom and Dad

In addition to Edward, there were two other guests at dinner that evening. One was Larry Leonard, an old friend of the family, and the other a young woman, Deborah, whom I had never met before. She was a native Vermonter, probably in her mid-20s, who had waited on my mother in a restaurant the previous week. When my mother learned that Deborah was living by herself in a local rooming house, she promptly invited her to dinner. Over the years, my mother had "rescued" any number of young men and women who seemed adrift and in need of love. Everyone adored my mother, but

14

few knew about her difficult childhood. Her father, a prominent physician, had started to abuse drugs and alcohol after sustaining a broken leg that had never healed properly. Without his steady income, my grandmother taught piano and took odd jobs to make ends meet. This left my mother, herself an adolescent, to raise her two younger siblings. The fact that she knew how it felt to have been abandoned by her own parents helped explain her desire to rescue other people. It was her way of embracing others and sharing the blessings of her life.

Sometimes, as with Deborah, the "rescue" was just for a meal; sometimes, strangers came to live with us for a year or two, whether in White Plains or Storm Acres. They were treated like members of the family, and often, even after getting back on their feet and moving away, these people remained our good friends.

This is how Larry Leonard came into our lives. My father had met him through work; he'd been invited for dinner a couple of times and then he came to stay with us in Storm Acres one summer while writing a book about politics and foreign policy. Mother used to joke that Larry never really left; I guessed he was here for at least a meal and probably for another couple of weeks.

As happened most nights when there were

guests, we ate in the dining room, which led by a swinging door to a mouse-proof pantry and then to a cramped, old-fashioned New England kitchen. The centerpiece of the kitchen was a large iron stove with an insulated compartment on one side just big enough to hold five or six burning logs that were used to cook the food and keep it warm. Before it was replaced by a gas stove, old "Ironsides" required every ounce of ingenuity and cunning my mother could muster to keep the fire burning hot enough to boil water on one corner of the stove, while simultaneously cooking a main dish here and warming two other dishes there. Sometimes there were just my parents for dinner; at other times, the number might swell to eight or ten, including unannounced relatives, friends, or a workman stopping by to fix the roof. Even when she'd planned a meal for four only to have the number seated at the dinner table jump to eight, there was always enough food for everyone. Entertaining and caring for others was her divine gift.

The night my friend Edward came to dinner we enjoyed a feast that was typical for late summer and the end of the ninety-day growing season. It was the time of year that gave my father the opportunity to show off the fruits of his backyard garden labors, which usually began in early May. With all of us sipping cocktails and seated comfortably around the roaring fire in the library, my father seized just the right moment to enter the room triumphantly, a big smile breaking out over his tanned face and his muscular arms full of freshly picked vegetables.

Listening to him brag about the pleasures of his garden reminded me of all the ways his life had been enriched by living in Vermont. Although he was then in his mid-sixties, he had the mental and physical agility of a much younger man. In college, he had done acrobatics, and although he wasn't an active sportsman as an adult, he'd watched his weight and kept himself in shape. After retiring to Storm Acres, he took up skiing and hiking and spent long hours each day tending to his garden and the many chores required to keep the house running. The rugged outdoor life in Vermont clearly agreed with him and no doubt contributed to his robust health, which lasted well into his nineties.

When it was finally time to eat, my father sat at the head of the table, and, as he had for years, served up food on everyone's plate while my mother, at the other end of the table, gently chided him for not giving just the right amount to each guest.

"Gordon," she said. "There's plenty more in the kitchen. Give Deborah another helping." Or, "Not so many potatoes for Larry, Gordon. He's trying to lose a few pounds."

Fortunately, it had been a favorable growing season, so in addition to the carrots, onions and squash, there was an abundance of my favorite Storm Acres vegetable: small-kernel sweet corn. Another special treat were the fat slices of juicy red tomatoes still warm from the afternoon sun. As delicious as these garden-to-table delicacies were, there was more to come. Dad had recently acquired several beehives, so we had local honey to spread on Mother's freshly baked cornbread.

For dessert, there was a choice of winter rhubarb or homemade ice cream covered with black raspberries and blueberries collected in the fields adjacent to the house. There was nothing fancy served at dinner that night and, certainly, nothing expensive. It was a meal that came straight from the humble Vermont soil and was offered up by two beloved spirits who had learned how to inherit the earth.

As usually happened when we had dinner guests, there was a lively discussion of politics—both national and global. Nixon's visit to China earlier in the year and the presidential prospects of George McGovern in November were debated at length; later, we moved on to talk about the violence and political unrest in Northern Ireland and the rumors that Pakistan had acquired the ability to build a nuclear bomb. I especially enjoyed hearing Larry Leonard's insider's gossip about Washington where he used to work for the government. But most of all, I loved to hear my father talk about politics. It was his life blood. In addition to getting involved in India's independence movement and being asked to leave the country, he'd led antiwar protests during the Vietnam War. He'd worked to support local and national Democratic candidates and even ran for mayor of White Plains on the Democratic ticket when I was in middle school. Whenever he felt strongly about an issue, he wrote letters to the editors of local and national newspapers which he eventually published in a memoir.

Connecting with Relatives and Friends

Through good times and bad, Storm Acres was a mecca for our extended family. Every few years, there were celebrations of the Honsinger, Halstead and Vernon clans. Honsinger was my mother's maiden name; in addition to her four siblings she had numerous aunts, uncles and cousins, all of whom had spouses and children of their own. Then there were other uncles and aunts, cousins and children who were all descendants, in one way or another, of my great grandfather Leroy Vernon. The Halstead side of the family included my brother, Scott and his wife, Edna—nicknamed Tot—and my sister, Welthy, and their children and spouses and grandchildren along with my father's two brothers and their offspring. But it didn't stop there because everyone had friends who wanted a slice of the Vermont magic. Sometimes there would be a throng of seventy or eighty spread out over the large front lawn, enjoying the summer sun and fresh mountain air. It was a chance to reconnect with people you hadn't seen in years or meet a distant relative whose name you'd often heard mentioned. People brought potluck dishes to share, and for those who wanted a little exercise, there were games like croquet or badminton on the front lawn or horseshoes out back.

My sister, Welthy Soni Myers

In the summer of 1978, in celebration of my

parents' 50th wedding anniversary, some of us put on a series of humorous skits depicting various events in their lives. Other years, there were weddings, birthdays and more anniversaries to celebrate. Always there were the intimate conversations that helped strengthen and enrich the fabric of our family bonds.

My brother, Scott Barker Halstead

At the center of each of these swirling, summer celebrations stood my parents, graceful and modest, my mother dressed in a colorful sari and my father standing proudly in his Nehru jacket, both of them slightly overwhelmed by what they had wrought. Yes, people came to celebrate them, but they also came to rediscover the glories of Storm Acres: the rolling hills swelling into mountains, the serenity of the nearby woods and the feeling of being connected to a simpler, nobler past that stretched back to the very founding of our nation.

Passing the Torch

Fortunately, my parents lived long enough that my two daughters (Larissa Vernon Halstead, born in 1975 and Christina deBosis Halstead born in 1977) got to know them in this bucolic setting and were able to absorb, over time, many of their values. They visited Storm Acres frequently enough at various seasons to discover their own secret pleasures and reasons for loving their grandparents' company.

One of the things that endeared them to their grandparents was their love of word games and cards. Both girls had quick, lively minds which made them good competitors, especially with my mother, in any kind of game. The game, *Oh, Hell*, was one of everyone's favorite. When someone had bad luck or simply got outplayed, it was permissible to shout out loud, "Oh, Hell!" Christina's and Larissa's love of competition and learning led us to play another game, called *Capitals*. It began with the state capitals and then, when they were mastered, we moved on to the capitals of foreign countries. One night at Storm Acres, while we were still at the dinner table and my parents were in the kitchen, I challenged them to a quick round of 'Capitals'. "The loser has to do the dishes," I said.

"Chile," I called out quickly while trying to watch both of them simultaneously. "Santiago," they said in unison.

"Good! How about Bolivia?" I said, not sure if they knew this one.

"That's too easy," Larissa said. She might have been bluffing. The next moment, Christina shouted, "La Paz."

"O.K.," I said. "Here's another easy one, Colombia."

"BO-GO-TA!" They chanted the three syllables while pounding out the rhythm on the table with their fists: "BO-GO-TA, BO-GO-TA," they repeated over and over to shouts of laughter.

Although they were close in age, with these games they were clever enough to adjust their expectations of each other so they could compete at a level that was both challenging and fun. It reflected a maturity and mutual respect that they have carried into adulthood and which has allowed them to remain best friends.

When they visited Storm Acres in winter, there was typically skiing at Mount Bromley or one of the mountains further north and snowshoeing in the meadows; in the summers, they could roam freely in the woods, escaping the hot and humid summers of Texas and, later,

Washington, DC. Their mother—my second wife, Margaret Gryzmkowski Halstead, but known as Kris—and I made every effort to help the girls spend at least part of their summers in Vermont so that they could go swimming in nearby Hapgood Pond and get lost in the woods searching for Mud Pond where they could fish, or just hang out. My mother also took the girls to the nearby town of Shaftsbury for horseback riding lessons.

At Storm Acres there was an endless variety of activities that didn't exist in the city: in the mornings, Larissa and Christina might get up early to pick wild blueberries for breakfast pancakes; later, they might help their grandfather weed the garden and pick vegetables for dinner; after lunch, they might bake cookies with their grandmother on the wood stove in the kitchen or help their mother cook a special dinner featuring Ukrainian dishes. In the evening, I might teach them how to build a fire in the fireplace.

Whenever we drove along back roads, my wife and I looked for farms where we might stop so the girls could talk with the farmers and see the cows being milked. When they were older, Larissa and Christina spent part of several summers at a nearby Quaker summer camp called Farm and Wilderness. Today, both girls are avid athletes and outdoorswomen; I like to believe this is due to those early experiences in Storm Acres.

As they have grown into accomplished adults, it's easy to see the blend of traits the girls inherited from their maternal and paternal grandparents as well as from their mother and myself. Larissa has developed a fierce commitment to social justice issues that informs her work in child welfare services, where she is widely admired for her intelligence and managerial skills; outside of work, she is equally esteemed for the way she gracefully and competently fulfills her many roles as mother, wife, daughter and homemaker. All skills that far exceed anything she learned from me.

Christina, by good fortune, has many of the same admirable traits. Elected Phi Beta Kappa in college, she then went on to earn a master's degree in international affairs, where she developed a passion for young people traumatized by war. This led to a brief excursion to Uganda where she engaged in activities to help child soldiers. When it became clear she would need a clinical degree to pursue this or related work, she had the courage and perseverance to take on a new challenge as an older student and pursue a master's in Social Work. Her commitment to excellence is apparent in everything she undertakes, which reassures her mother and me that she will excel in whatever path she chooses.

My son, Alexander Vivante Halstead, born in 1992 to my third and present wife, Jessica Scheer Halstead, has enjoyed his own unique experience of Storm Acres. Although by the time Alex was born my father no longer had the energy to keep up with an active boy, there were still many places they explored together.

The old barn, which was attached to one wing of the house, had a workbench with a lot of interesting, old-fashioned tools. Previous owners had kept horses in the barn, which meant there were stalls with harnesses and a hayloft to climb into. Porcupines had eaten away some of the beams which supported the roof and there were traces of other wild animals like deer, fox and possum, who had visited the barn. Behind the house, my father had his beloved vegetable garden and he explained to Alex with pride which vegetables grew best in the Vermont soil and the various strategies used to keep away the deer, rabbits, voles and squirrels.

*On top of Mt. Stratton in Southern Vermont
with Alexander, 1997.*

I showed Alex how to build fires in the library fireplace, and Jessica took him hiking in the woods, stopping in the back yard to pick apples and inspect the beehives. At other times, his grandmother read him adventure stories on the side porch and told him about the early days of Storm Acres when there was no telephone or TV.

When the air was warm and the sun was shining at Storm Acres, Jessica and I took Alex to Hapgood Pond, where he loved to splash in the shallow area and dig in the sand with his shovel and pail. Even from a distance, I could spot his blond hair and hear his excited squeals as he waded into the deep, unexpectedly cold water. Later, the three of us would spread out a blanket under a tree overlooking the water and enjoy a leisurely picnic lunch. During those formative years, everyone could see the young man he would become: his bright, inquisitive mind and his tall, athletic build. From an early age, he loved gadgets and building things. Playing with Legos was a particular favorite, and we used to sit on the floor in front of the fire for hours challenging each other to see who could build the tallest or fanciest structures.

In the time Alex had with his grandparents, his mother and I did our best to convey the enduring values their lives reflected, and I believe he came to understand how these values were enhanced by the beauty and solitude of Storm Acres.

*My parents, Helen and Gordon, relaxing on
the side porch swing.*

Dying of the Light

In the first few years after the new millennium, my father had the first of several minor strokes. He was in his mid-90s—nearly as old as the century—and at that age living year-round at Storm Acres required heroic strength and endurance, especially in winter. The house was also showing its age and was in constant need of costly repairs. It was too much for an elderly couple who were in need of their own repairs. Yet, saying goodbye to Storm Acres felt like a little death. It had been an intimate part of their lives, and ours, since 1938: a still point in a spinning world. My parents had not changed the course of history, but they had played their part, and played it well. It was time to say goodbye to Storm Acres.

My siblings, Scott and Welthy, and I decided to step in before something catastrophic happened. We put the house on the market, and Welthy found them a comfortable apartment in an assisted living complex down in the valley near Bennington. My father died first, peacefully in his sleep, at the age of ninety-eight. My mother, who maintained her vigor and sense of humor until the last few months, died seven years later at the age of 103. In accordance with their wishes, their ashes were buried in a small plot on Storm Acres adjacent to one of the golden meadows they loved so much. Their passing was sad but not unexpected. They had both lived long, full lives and there was much to be thankful for, much to celebrate.

Before the house and land were sold, two subplots were split off to keep in the family. Scott and his wife, Tot, and their children own a small house on one of these plots, which is used mostly for vacations. My sister and her husband, Paul, have built an energy-efficient, mostly off-the-grid house on the other plot, where they live most of the year. Their house is a modern bookend to the original Storm Acres house which was also 'off the grid' for many years. Although it's difficult to replicate all the features of Storm Acres that made it special, at least the continued presence of my brother and sister and their families make it possible to hold family reunions and experience once again the wonders of dwelling among the ancestral mountains. When it's difficult for me to return physically to this land which has had a mystical hold on me for most of my life, I visit Storm Acres through the magic of this poem.

Family and friends at a Storm Acres summer gathering.

STORM ACRES

When to my heart a darkness comes
And sadness seals its spell;
I turn to thee, O verdant god,
And seek thy cradled dell.

On easeful waves of inward sight
I'm carried to thy side,
A distant farm in green clad hills,
Unknown, my boyhood bride.

A bride who knew no sovereign sorrow
Or paled with earthly years,
I lived in tender happiness
Sealed off from human fears.

An oasis in a weary waste
Whose spring I never found,
Yet, imbibed my very being
As I shared the shaded ground.

Ah, verdant youth knew not what wealth
The birches could have taught,
But, while in secret glade I played
Unaware my soul was bought.

When to my heart a darkness comes
And sorrow clouds my eyes,
I turn to thee, O verdant god,
To seek thy paradise.

Lauro Halstead, 1956

Flying to Foreign Lands

Chapter One:
A Summer Rendezvous

It was going to be an ideal summer. In 1954, following my freshman year at Haverford College, I sailed to Europe, where I spent two weeks hitchhiking through England and Scotland before traveling on to France. Although I wanted to see as much of Europe as possible, my main goal was to improve my French, so I had made arrangements with my French professor, Laurence Wylie, to live with a family in southern France for July and August.

Wylie had given me a letter of introduction to the family, with whom he had also lived. My professor had just published a popular book about postwar rural life in southern France, which was set in the fictional village of Peyrane. "Not too many people speak English there, but your French is good enough to get by," Wylie told me. "It'll be a great summer rendezvous."

My career plans were still vague, but the idea of a job with the Foreign Service was appealing. Maybe this family would have a pretty daughter and we would fall in love. That would

36

certainly help my French. Yes, everything was going to be ideal.

But I never made it to the French village.

While I was in Paris, in the elevator going up the Eiffel Tower, I ran into Tom Padden, an American tourist I'd met on the boat to Europe. Tom was in his mid-20's, with an easy-going Midwestern confidence that made him an ideal travel companion, so we decided to hitchhike to southern France together. But when we got as far as Chartres, I had a chance encounter that changed our travel plans and the rest of my life. I was in the great cathedral of Chartres, admiring the rose window, when a short, rather stocky gentleman who was standing next to me asked, "Are you American?" Before I could answer, he said, "I am Francisco da Cunha. I am from Oporto, Portugal."

I introduced myself and we shook hands.

Francisco told me that for several years he'd been the wrestling champion of Portugal. He was also, he said, a great admirer of America. "I especially like your president, Mr. Roosevelt. He's a great man." Francisco had visited relatives in New York City before the war.

We chatted for a few minutes about the war and life in America. I mentioned that during the war my parents had been invited to dinner with Mrs. Roosevelt at the White House to discuss ideas my father had for helping Chinese refugees immigrate to this country. The president had been occupied and had not attended the dinner. Nevertheless, Francisco was impressed.

"I love Roosevelt. Everyone love Roosevelt," Francisco said. "He won the war for us. I love America and democracy. In Portugal, no democracy. We only have Salazar, Mr. Big Dictator."

Francisco was part of a group of Portuguese tourists exploring France by chartered bus. Now they were returning home to Portugal.

"If you boys want ride, we have empty seats," Francisco said. "Come with us to the Spanish frontier." As we walked toward the bus, the sky suddenly darkened and a heavy rain fell. Tom and I got soaked, but once we were on the bus, the other passengers befriended us and helped us to dry off. By the end of the day, Francisco had convinced us to stay on board all the way to Portugal.

Tom and I spent a week relaxing at Francisco's ocean-side home in Oporto before catching a train to Madrid. Our plan was to make a quick stop in the Spanish capital before I would move on to the village in southern France.

In Madrid we headed to a cheap *pension* which, according to our guidebook, was not far from where Hemingway had stayed in the 1930's. But before I could even climb the stairs to our tiny room on the third floor, I started to feel ill: my neck was stiff and I had a pounding headache. Later that evening, I developed diarrhea and a high fever.

Turista, I thought. *I must have picked up a bug in Portugal.* But at some level, I knew this wasn't *turista*. I had never felt this sick before and by the end of my first day in Madrid, my right arm had become weak and my legs felt heavy.

"I just need a good night's sleep," I said to Tom, who didn't look reassured. "We'll be on the road again in no time," I added, still determined to meet up with that pretty French daughter I'd imagined.

Inside our room, the Spanish midday sun made the air stagnant and thick. It was difficult to suck any into my lungs.

With a growing sense of dread, I wondered what was wrong with my right arm. I couldn't lift it. I drifted in and out of consciousness. I tried to focus on the flowers on the colorful wall paper next to my bed. Or were they fruit? I wasn't sure.

"Wasn't it just this morning that I brought the washcloth up to my face?" I wondered aloud. Perhaps it had been yesterday. And my legs: "How had I managed to climb the stairs when now I couldn't move them across the sheets?" I was terrified.

With some effort, I brought my left hand to

my face. "See that?" I asked Tom, who may or may not have been in the room. So at least my arm still worked, I thought, relieved. "But what about tomorrow? Whatever it is, this thing is moving fast."

I scratched my nose and realized how good it felt. Touching my face had somehow made me more lucid. "Good God!" I heard myself cry out. "Help me! Help me!" And then, in a whisper, "If I can't use my left arm, I'll be totally paralyzed." Fear closed in, suffocating my breath even more.

Tom was scared, too, but to hide it he turned his back and started to sing in a low voice, "The old grey mare, she ain't what she used to be, she ain't..."

"Don't worry." I cut him off with all the strength I could muster. "I'm not an old grey mare. I've been sick before. Let me tough it out. I still want to rendezvous in France."

Tom turned serious. He sat on a chair close to my bed. "I know you're tough but let me tell you what I've been thinking. There's a big American airbase outside of town." His calm, practical, Kansas farm-boy demeanor soothed me. He'd just gotten off the phone with Dr. William Patterson, the physician on call at the Air Force hospital. Unfortunately, I couldn't be admitted because I wasn't in the military. But the doctor had promised to call a Spanish physician in the morning who could treat me.

Later that night, maybe 2 or 3 in the morning, there was a commotion outside the bedroom door. Then a tall, older American came into the room. It was Dr. Patterson.

"I couldn't sleep worrying about your condition," he said. "I told my wife you're an American citizen and you need help." He paused, carefully considering his next words. "I told her the military be damned! So here I am." He asked me some questions and then spent a few moments examining me.

"You're damn sick, you know," he said in a husky voice. I could smell cigarettes on his breath. "I don't need any damn tests to know you have classic paralytic polio which means your European adventure is over. I know an excellent Spanish physician. I'll call him in the morning and ask him to put you in a hospital."

It's hard to remember now the fear caused by the very word "polio." Epidemics swept the United States and other developed countries during the 1930's, '40's and '50's, causing panic, paralysis and death. In 1952, the worst year on record in the U.S., over 52,000 cases were diagnosed. Some called it the summer plague, as there was a spike in the number of cases during warm months. For some of those years it became the most common cause of death among young children, leading to the mistaken idea that it didn't affect adults. While it was known that the disease was caused by a virus, it was not widely understood how it was transmitted. Many people avoided crowded movie theaters or swimming pools. Some wealthy families even sent their children away, to mountain resorts or to the Caribbean islands. Europe in the summer of 1954 seemed as safe a place as any.

In my delirium, Dr. Patterson disappeared into shadowy blackness. Hours seemed to pass. When I opened my eyes, the doctor was still there.

"I don't like your breathing, kiddo," he said. "You're going to need respiratory assistance. If you were in the States, I'd put you in an iron lung pronto." He paused to let his words sink in as I tried to absorb what I couldn't believe. This was a veteran officer used to being blunt. "Unfortunately, there aren't any iron lungs in this godforsaken country. But I've heard they have a wooden lung in the local children's hospital. I'll try to get you in there before I go off duty at 0800 hours." It seemed like he was speaking to me now from a room down the hall. I thought it strange, but didn't have the strength to utter a single word. I was barely breathing.

*****

When I came to the following morning, my 6-foot-4 frame was stuffed into a wooden lung, a plywood contraption made for someone much smaller. I have since seen pictures of the Spanish version of the iron lung: a large wooden crate with a small electric motor on one end, which pumped air in and out of the person lying inside.

Whoosh: the air was sucked into my lungs, and as the motor turned the pump, *woo:* there was a fainter rumble as air was exhaled from my lungs, through my throat and finally past my teeth. In and out. In and out. Hour after hour I lay motionless while the respirator did the work of keeping me alive.

I was in *El Hospital Del Niño Jesus*, a Catholic hospital built in the 17th or 18th century and staffed by nuns from the *Hijas de la Caridad* order, who weren't allowed to touch the adult male body. My room was in the basement—their idea of an isolation ward, I suppose—which had tall ceilings covered with frescoes of baby Jesus frolicking with children who all looked like Goldilocks. I was the sole patient in that room, flat on my back, my gaze fixated on the frescoes high above my head, my knees pressed against my chest in the cramped wooden lung, which wheezed and swooshed. There was no call bell or way to alert someone if I needed help. To the nuns, my body was a mere ephemeral vessel; what was important was my eternal soul.

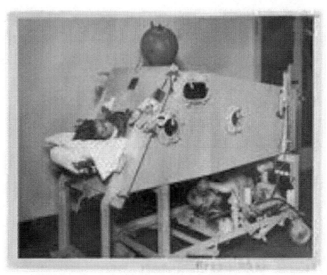

Wooden respirator of the type that saved my life.

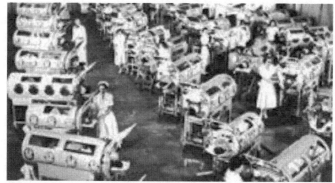

Iron lungs in a U.S. polio respiratory center in the early 1950's.

When they weren't singing and praying in a courtyard adjacent to the basement, the nuns treated me like a prized catch.

"Qué buena suerte," I heard them say to one another. What good luck. I suppose they meant that I was lucky to be in the hospital, but I felt helpless and trapped as the young nuns stood around me, laughing and bantering. My freshman Spanish wasn't good enough to understand most of their chatter. But when they became serious, I didn't have any difficulty catching their meaning: God in his wisdom had chosen this illness and delivered me to them so they might save my soul. Indeed, why was I not more grateful? I tried to think what sins had brought me so low.

One afternoon, a short, plump priest stopped by my bed. "The nuns are praying for you around the clock," he said in English. Then, making the sign of the cross, he added, "But it is only I who can hear your confession and convert you into the true faith." I thanked him but said I wasn't ready to become a Catholic yet.

A few days later, a miracle did happen: My mother arrived from America. "I've never been a nurse," she said, "but I've raised three kids and know how to make myself useful." It was a characteristic understatement. Since the nuns were in charge of my soul, she took charge of my body. She gave me a daily bed bath and placed wonderful-smelling flowers close to my head. I had difficulty swallowing but she somehow managed to track down ingredients in the

Spanish markets that were easy to swallow and appealed to my teenaged palate. But the best nourishment was her presence. We talked about everything: girls, college, movies, books, friends, politics, and, of course, going home. She read aloud from books and magazines she'd brought. She read an entire novel, *The Citadel*, by A.J. Cronin as well as a piece from the *Reader's Digest* entitled, *"Turning Your Stumbling Blocks into Stepping Stones."* We discussed the meaning of this article for a long time and concluded that no matter how big a stumbling block my illness was, we would find ways to turn it into a stepping stone. The priest could not have found a more profound and inspiring message. In the years that followed, it became a guiding metaphor for me during many of life's travails.

Late one night the electricity failed, and the wooden lung suddenly stopped working. Deprived of oxygen, I began to writhe in a kind of convulsion. I felt as though blunt knives were piercing my skin, twisting hard into my muscles. I prayed for a comfortable bed.

"Por favor, por favor," I screamed without breath. *"Ayúdame!*—Help me! It was barely a whisper. In my oxygen-deprived stupor, I prayed again for a comfortable bed. And suddenly, there it was. Baby Jesus had answered my prayers. On the far side of the darkened room I could see a four-poster bed, with large

down pillows and a soft mattress. "Oh, Lord. *Gracias*. Thank you, Jesus." I called for someone to carry me to this bed. No one came, and in a flash the phantom bed was gone. The power had come back on. Beautiful, fresh oxygen filled my lungs and my muscles relaxed.

The nuns, who had been praying in the nearby courtyard, rushed in to see if their prayers had worked. The pain was gone and the respirator was breathing for me again. Did I dare tell the keepers of my soul that I was back in heaven? What would they think of a heaven that was simply pain-free and no bigger than a working respirator?

And then it happened again. And again. Every night, from 2 to 6 AM, the power grid all over the Spanish capital shut down, robbing me of the trickle of electrons needed to keep me alive. These outages, I later learned, were on the orders of the Spanish dictator, Francisco Franco, whose fascist regime was on a life support of its own.

Somewhere in the midst of this living hell—I wasn't sure if it was day or night—the English-speaking priest appeared out of a shadow and sat by the respirator. As usual, I was lying on my back with only my head sticking out of the respirator. The priest waited a few moments, as though making sure we were alone, and then brought his lips close to my right ear. "The doctor says he's discouraged," he said.

"Your prognosis is poor." Now his wet tongue was brushing up against my ear. "In fact, the doctor says you might leave this earth any—" His voice dropped so low it was lost in the mechanical noise of the respirator. *Whoosh, woo, whoosh, woo.* Then in a louder voice, "It is my duty, Lauro Halstead, to give you last rites, here and now. It's your only chance to be saved." *Last rites!* I was incensed. I waited for the respirator to fill my lungs with air, then as I exhaled I whispered with all my might, "No ... Go to hell! ... Leave me alone!"

On my eighteenth day in Madrid, Dr. Patterson came to my rescue again. Through his contacts at the air base, he organized a mercy flight that took me from Spain to an American military hospital in Wiesbaden, Germany. From there, I was flown to a hospital near our home outside New York City. My parents put aside any angry and bitter feelings they might have had about my misfortune and hailed my return to the States as a triumph—especially my mother, who knew how sick I had been, and how the helping hands of strangers such as Tom Padden and Dr. Patterson had reached out to keep me alive and get me safely home. Tom had left Madrid shortly after my mother's arrival. Now I wrote to thank him for the critical role he'd played in saving my life, and we exchanged letters for a year or two before losing touch.

In 1964, ten years after my illness, when I had graduated from medical school and was working in a hospital in Washington, DC, I happened to sit down in the cafeteria for lunch one day across the table from an attractive surgical intern. As we chatted, I learned that she was the daughter of an Army surgeon and had once lived in Madrid.

I told her about my Madrid misadventure, and asked if by any chance she remembered meeting a Dr. William Patterson, who'd worked at the US airbase there in the early 1950's.

"Dr. Patterson!" she exclaimed. "Oh, my God! He's my father!"

Dr. Patterson was retired and lived a few miles away, in Northern Virginia. The following week, I invited him, his wife and daughter to join me and my parents, who came down from New York, for a reunion dinner in my apartment in Georgetown. There I had the opportunity to thank Dr. Patterson for saving my life as well as for inspiring me to pursue a career in medicine.

On my first pass from the U.S. hospital, October 1954.

*****

It had not been the summer I had expected. But I had survived. Over the next six months, my breathing slowly improved, my legs became strong enough to walk and I learned to write with my left hand. By January 1955, I was well enough to leave the hospital and return home for a few weeks before heading back to college.

One of the first visitors to our house was my beloved grandmother. I was happy to see her, though I became increasingly dismayed as she went on and on about how lucky I had been. "God in His wisdom has chosen you," she said. "He knows you are strong and He gives you only what you can bear."

Lucky. A lot of people told me that I was lucky to be alive, not realizing how it sounded to someone still in his late teens. I didn't feel at all lucky to be paralyzed for the rest of my life. Later, though, I realized there were other ways of thinking about it. If I was destined to get polio, better to get it at 18 with a fully grown skeleton. It also meant I was able to enjoy the carefree years of childhood and was able to play sports and develop my body in normal ways right up through my first year in college. In high school, I'd spent a summer on a Navajo reservation in Arizona, helping to build a house and a small medical clinic. None of that would have been possible if I'd had a severe case of polio as an infant or young child. Later still, I realized that if I hadn't had polio, I might not have chosen to attend medical school and had a fulfilling career in medicine.

I couldn't agree with my grandmother about being chosen. What about people who bore even greater burdens than I—those who ended up permanently in an iron lung, for example? Were they luckier still, because God in His wisdom had chosen them for that cruel fate? But instead of engaging my grandmother in a pointless debate, I simply thanked her for her prayers and good wishes.

When I finally returned to college, I was confronted with entirely different reactions to my illness. "You look phenomenal," one classmate told me, as we walked to class. "You don't look or act disabled at all. I bet you can do anything you want."

He meant it kindly, but his comment put me in an unpleasant bind: Did I want to accept his judgment and pretend I was "normal" or did I want to be honest and insist that people realize I had certain limitations? Over a period of several months, I worked out a compromise: I was completely open and honest with my closest friends. With the rest of the universe I tried to "pass" and let them believe I wasn't disabled. So I let my roommates and other close friends know exactly what I couldn't do. I asked for help with simple, two-handed tasks such as tying my necktie or cutting a thick piece of meat, and avoided activities that stressed my legs such as dancing or walking two miles into town on Saturday night for a beer.

When it was time to choose a profession, medicine suddenly had a special appeal. I'd considered a career in medicine before college, but without any particular enthusiasm. Polio changed all that, exposing me to two informal, specialized "schools." In the first, I learned what it was like to be a patient, to be sick, completely helpless, a few breaths away from death.

In the second school, I learned a great deal about those who practice the art of healing. There are many types of physicians, but the ones I was drawn to were those whose very presence at the bedside made one feel better. As I lay in bed week after week, I had plenty of time to observe these doctors closely and try to understand what made them special. After I became a physician, they were my role models. When I applied to medical school, I tried to turn my illness and disability into an asset. I may not have been as good a student of chemistry and biology as the others, but I had the advantage of having already graduated from two specialized schools—before a single med school class had begun—that taught me the nuances of being both a patient and a doctor. My healthy body was lost, but in that loss I uncovered new sources of inspiration and resilience.

Chapter Two:
Phoenix Rising

On the last day of July 1957, I set out to climb Mount Fuji with Akira Iriye, a Japanese friend from college. I'd just finished my junior year and was spending three months in Japan on a work-study fellowship grant from the American Friends Service Committee. My bout with polio, now three years in the past, had weakened both legs, but I decided that the climb would be an exciting challenge.

At over 12,300 feet, Fuji is the tallest mountain in the Japanese islands, a majestic inactive volcano whose almost-perfect symmetry is enhanced by a crown of snow. For centuries, Fujisan, as it is affectionately called, has been the holiest site of the Shinto religion. Devout Japanese try to climb it at least once in their lifetimes, but even for a non-disabled person, it is an arduous journey.

*****

Although Akira had never climbed the mountain, he was no stranger to challenges. As a child growing up in Tokyo during the war, he'd survived on a meager diet and witnessed firebombing that destroyed houses in his neighborhood. At college, his extreme reserve suggested indolence, but he was probably the smartest student in our class, and he would eventually win the top prizes in history and mathematics at graduation.

During the two years we were roommates, we'd talked a lot about Japan. "I'd like to show you all my favorite places," he'd said once during sophomore year, as we looked at one of his family albums full of grainy black and white photographs. "My parents would love to have you stay with us. You would bring great honor on our house." Then he pointed to a picture of Mt Fuji he had taken from the roof of his parents' home. "I've always wanted to climb Fuji-san," Akira said. "If you think you're strong enough, we can climb it together."

Snowcapped Mt. Fuji. on a Spring day

Although his parents had lived in Europe, they maintained traditional Japanese gender roles. His mother cooked while kneeling on the floor of a tiny kitchen, eating only after the men in the family had finished. The household had a small wooden bathtub which was filled only once each night. As the honored guest, I was instructed to use it first, when the water was still boiling hot. Then it was Akira's turn to bathe, followed by his father, his mother, and finally, his elderly grandmother.

A tour bus took Akira and me up above the tree line to an altitude of 7500 feet. Gazing up at the snowcapped peak more than a mile above my head, I felt a sharp tingle at the base of my spine and an unpleasant chill in my legs that made them shake.

I hadn't slept well the night before, and I'd awoken a little before dawn, my legs aching and my forehead hot. Was I getting sick again? Although my doctors had said I'd made a good recovery, I hadn't faced a challenge like this one.

"I'm worried about my legs," I finally confided to Akira. "It's a long way to the top."

My friend assured me that we'd go slowly. Despite its height, climbing Fuji doesn't require any special equipment—a well-worn, winding footpath leads all the way to the top. Experienced climbers reach the summit in six to eight hours; novices are told to allow at least twelve. We began our ascent at four in the afternoon, planning to climb all night and reach the summit in time for the sunrise at 4:30.

As we passed the 8000-foot marker, I became increasingly aware of the religious nature of the journey. The path became a flowing column of humanity—hundreds, maybe thousands of people were moving slowly, implacably, towards the heavens. The vast majority of the pilgrims were elderly, many bent with age. The climb is thought to bring spiritual cleansing as well as physical healing. I tried to feel the energy of the people around me and let myself be carried along by their faith.

Somewhere near 9000 feet, my breathing

became labored and I realized my body was struggling for oxygen. I flashed back to my time in the artificial lung in the *Hospital del Niño Jesus* in Madrid. "What if I can't breathe?" I gasped. My head was spinning. "Akira, what will I do?" He didn't answer. I realized that he wasn't next to me anymore—I saw his red plaid shirt up ahead in a small group of people clustered around a motionless figure on the ground. A short time later, two men hurried down the mountain path bearing a stretcher. On it was a man not much older than I, pale and still. Someone near me whispered, "Heart attack. Happens all the time." At that I bent over, clutching my chest, gasping for air. The tips of my fingers tingled. An elderly woman saw my distress and said, with a gentle smile across empty gums, "No breathe fast."

At 10,000 feet, the path became steeper and the air much colder. Small chunks of brown volcanic rock littered the path. I'd heard about people slipping on these rocks and disappearing over the edge of the trail. Akira and I slowed our pace and took breaks every 30 or 40 feet. With every step, my body felt heavier, my knees more painful.

"This is tougher than I expected," I finally admitted to Akira. We were enveloped in a thick band of clouds which blocked our vision and covered us with a fine mist. "You go ahead and I'll wait for you here."

"No chance," he replied without hesitating. "We're going to make it together." It seemed that none of the elderly Japanese around us were affected by the steeper climb, the dropping temperature and the thinning air. Their perseverance gave me the courage to push on.

Since arriving in this country, I'd learned a lot about Japanese perseverance. Riding around Tokyo in a taxi on my first day in Japan, I'd wondered where all the rubble from the war was. The streets were clogged with cars and well-dressed people; there were construction cranes everywhere. It was hard to imagine that only nine years earlier, napalm and incendiary bombs had destroyed vast swaths of wooden housing in the city and killed over 100,000 people. Japan was making an extraordinary recovery from the greatest catastrophe of its thousand-year history. "Phoenix Rising from the Ashes," was the way one American newspaper headline put it.

Now, it seemed that Akira and I were also experiencing a kind of rebirth.

When we reached 10,500 feet, I began to hear a low hum. What sounded at first like the wind proved to be a religious chant.

"They are Shintoists," Akira said. "They're trying to communicate with their ancestors." He added, "They're also praying for strength to make it safely to the top." The chanting and determination of the hundreds of pilgrims around us stirred my soul. I felt that this mountain was inhabited by powerful, ancient gods. I took a deep breath. My legs felt lighter and the cold air refreshed my face.

When we reached 11,000 feet, we had been climbing in the dark for several hours. It was nearly 1 AM and we were above the clouds. We had a thousand feet still to climb in order to make it to the top by sunrise. I turned and looked back down the mountain path, where climbers carrying lanterns and flashlights made a zigzagging string of blinking lights, whose tail disappeared into the clouds below. Now we were taking rest breaks every ten or fifteen feet. Akira was panting as heavily as I was.

At 11,500 feet I entered a state of oblivion, maybe caused by muscle pain or lack of sleep. I was probably also suffering from altitude sickness. I don't have any clear memory of the last part of the climb. According to Akira, we just kept at it, one heavy step after the other. Suddenly, I was standing next to the Shinto shrine at the summit, trying to make a snowball. To the east a faint light was moving up the valley that stretched out far below. Tokyo was on the edge of the horizon. "We made it," I whispered, exhausted and dazed. "We made it." We hugged as much for warmth as for joy. "I could never have done it without you," I told Akira. Still struggling to think clearly, I asked him what the date was.

"August first," he replied.

Then it hit me. *Today is exactly three years to the day since I got sick with polio.* With tears of joy I lifted my eyes to the heavens. It had been a long journey from Madrid to the top of Mount Fuji. And I had made it.

Chapter Three:
Reading Dante

One morning in early October 1958, I dragged a bulging, brown leather suitcase up the gang-plank of the Italian ocean liner *Cristoforo Colombo,* bound for Genoa, Italy—Christopher Columbus's hometown. As I stood at the railing waving goodbye to my parents on the pier below, I shouted into the wind in Italian, "*Sono molto fortunato.*" I'm very lucky.

Above the ship in the cool October air, I could see the New York skyline with its tall, proud buildings reaching up toward eternity. *This is my chance to reach for the heavens,* I thought. *I'm young, single and about to live in Rome for a year.*

I'd graduated from Haverford in June and my plan—if I was accepted—was to enter medical school in the fall of 1959. In the meantime, I was setting out to study Italian literature at the University of Rome.

"If you want to become a physician, why take a year off to live in Italy?" people often asked me. "Wouldn't it make more sense to work in a lab or take extra pre-med courses?"

Well, yes, it would have made more sense. But going to Italy for a year wasn't the result of hard logic. Rather, it was a journey of the heart, a journey that may have begun when my parents gave me my first name, Lauro, and my second name, deBosis. I don't have any Italian blood, but I was named for Lauro deBosis, an Italian war hero—related to my mother by marriage—who died fighting fascism.

My name didn't seem especially unusual until the eighth grade, when a friend started to make fun of it saying things like, "Lauro, Laurie, Lee, Lee." At twelve, you don't want to be different, so instead of being proud of my name, I found it deeply embarrassing: *Why did my parents have to give me a funny name that no one has heard of? Why couldn't they have just called me George or Frederick after one of my grandfathers?*

At the same time, kids making fun of my name made me feel special; it connected me with something bigger and intangible outside of myself.

Then one day during 11th grade at Andover, one of my favorite teachers, Mr. Wallace, stopped me after class. Phillips Academy or Andover is a private boarding school outside of Boston.

"I noticed your first name," he said. "Where did you get it? There was a famous Italian patriot named Lauro deBosis who died fighting Mussolini and fascism," he continued. "I think he was also a poet. Have you ever heard of him?"

It turned out that Mr. Wallace, a scholar and respected teacher of European history, knew all about Lauro deBosis and thought highly of him. Filled with pride, for the first time I saw my name as a badge of honor. Of course my parents had thought Lauro was a great man, but he was a relative. Now, someone outside our family knew who he was and what he had done. "Lauro," I whispered to myself. "What a great name. Lucky for me I wasn't just named Joe."

Soon after this encounter, Mr. Wallace and his wife, Angela, an Italian-American, invited me to their home for an old-fashioned Italian meal.

"This is called *minestra di fagioli*," Mrs. Wallace said as she placed a bowl of bean soup in front of me. She was younger than her husband, maybe in her mid-thirties, with long black hair and a *bella figura*. While I was finishing the soup, Mrs. Wallace said in a confidential whisper, "Please call me Angelina. All my friends do."

"Yes, ma'am," I said. I was thrilled. Andover was still a boys' school in those days, so having an attractive female dinner companion, even if she was married, was a special treat.

During the main course of homemade linguini and clam sauce, I told my hosts what I knew about my illustrious relative: He was born in 1901 in Rome, the son of a businessman and a fairly prominent poet named Adolfo deBosis. Lauro's mother, Lillian, was an American, whose sister was my maternal grandmother. The sisters had been born in Rome to American parents; Lillian had stayed in Italy after marrying

Adolpho deBosis, while her sister, Evalina, had moved back to America and married my grand-father. Thus their daughter, Helen—my mother—was Lauro deBosis' first cousin.

I could see that the Wallaces were confused by all this family history, so I borrowed a pencil and sketched out on a paper napkin the relevant portion of my family tree.

After examing it for a moment, Angelina, who had studied art history in Florence, said, "Okay. I think we've got it straight now." She flashed me a Mona Lisa smile. "Go ahead with your story."

"Lauro was a kind of prodigy," I continued. "He received a classical education and translated several Greek plays into Italian. He also won the top prize in poetry for Italy at the 1928 Olympic Games in Amsterdam. In those days, besides sports, they gave prizes to young authors."

Angelina rose to clear the table for dessert, and I feared that I was boring these nice people with too many details.

But I needn't have worried. "Wasn't he a leader in fighting Mussolini?" Angelina asked.

"That's true," I said. I explained that at first, after the Olympics, Lauro was the darling of the fascist government. But, as he learned more about politics, he came to detest the corrupt and distorted underbelly of fascism. Together with some friends, he started an underground party, the *Alleanza Nazionale*, to overthrow Mussolini. In an effort to publicize this tiny party's efforts and to gain more popular support, Lauro piloted a small plane over Rome in October 1931, dropping leaflets on the people below.

"Mussolini's planes shot him down," I said. "He was only thirty years old." I paused, and as I resumed, I could feel my face flush with pride: "After the war, the Italian government placed a bust of Lauro on one of the hills of Rome, together with other heroes of Italian history. He is the only Italian of the twentieth century to receive this honor."

My audience was clearly impressed. At the same time, telling Lauro's story made me feel, in some mysterious way, that a small part of his glory had rubbed off on me. Is it any wonder that one day I'd want to live in his shadow?

Angelina leaned over and touched my hand. "It's a marvelous story, and for you, a wonderful heritage."

Over the years, I've had countless opportunities to tell the story of Lauro's life. And every time, I've felt the same surge of pride to know that I was named for such a man. But such encounters hadn't yet led to fantasies of sailing to Italy or studying Italian. Actually, throughout high school and my first year in college, I was determined to master French and even began studying Spanish with an eye towards a career in the Foreign Service.

That dream quickly disappeared after I contracted polio. When I finally returned to Haverford, I enrolled in a first-year Italian class at nearby Bryn Mawr. But I wasn't thinking about a year abroad. Rather, life had suddenly seemed terribly fragile and I'd decided it was time to embrace my Italian heritage.

But fate was steering me toward Italy. One day in early fall during my third year in college, Aldo Caselli called me into his office. Mr Caselli was an Italian economist who'd fled Italy during the war and landed a job as the college comptroller; he was also in charge of building maintenance.

"Why you write your initials on my bedroom door?" he asked me. I lived in one of the school dormitory suites with three classmates, and each of us had a separate bedroom labelled A, B, C and D. Mine was labeled with the letter 'B' and in honor of my middle name, I'd written the letters 'de' to make 'deB' for deBosis in black felt-tip pen.

No one had noticed that I had defaced school property until now. Mr. Caselli was in his mid-40's, balding and rather stocky. *He's seen a lot of pasta*, I thought.

"I not upset that you write on my door. We can make to disappear," he said. He waved his arms up and down as if erasing a blackboard. "What I wanna know, is it because your middle name, deBosis?"

Bingo! Of course it was. And as an Italian who

was familiar with the antifascist struggle, Mr. Caselli knew about Lauro's heroic flight and death. As we talked, I mentioned I had taken a year of Italian at Bryn Mawr but couldn't do a second year because of schedule conflicts.

"Why donna you take private class with me?" He asked. "I teach you everything."

For the next year and a half we met twice a week in his office. He didn't teach me everything, but he taught me a lot; it was one of the best learning experiences of my life.

"The key to speak the Italian is to master the vowels," he said during our first session. "Not like the English, Italian vowels they almost never change." His English vowels faithfully followed Italian rules.

"For example, 'a' is pronounce like the first 'a' in papa, like, you see in Italian word for bread '*pane*'. Now you try."

Patiently, word by word, phrase by phrase, he coached me through the basics of good Italian pronunciation. His goal was to rid my speech of an American accent and bring me closer to sounding like a native speaker. At one point, to wash out my American sounds, we went outside, where he had me scream Italian poetry as loudly as I could. It was a miraculous exercise. When I brought my voice down to a conversational level, my pronunciation magically sounded more authentic.

"*Va bene, va bene*, okay, okay," he said one

day. He was very excited. "Your Italian pronunciation is *molto bene*. I call my wife. She gonna like what you say."

He had me say a few words and phrases to his Italian wife over the phone. She congratulated me and said I sounded like I came from northern Italy. In addition to giving me a great accent, he also had me memorize his favorite stanzas from Dante's *Inferno,* always reciting them at the top of my lungs. It was an extraordinary gift. During our last class together, Mr. Caselli gave me an illustrated copy of Dante's poetry as a graduation present.

Although I had made up my mind to pursue a career in medicine, as my Italian improved, the idea of living in Italy for a year became more and more attractive.

"It'll give me a chance to know my Italian relatives," I used to tell my friends. "Also, I like the idea of living in a different culture and becoming more fluent in a second language." The dilemma was: when should I do it? After college and before medical school seemed to make the most sense. It might make getting into medical school more difficult, but I would have to take the risk.

As a final preparation for my year in Italy, my maternal grandmother, Evalina, came to live with us for the three months leading up to my trip on the *Cristoforo Colombo*. Born in Rome, Evalina had moved to America when she was fifteen. Italian was her first language and she retained her fluency into old age. She was a tall, elegant woman with posture that would have pleased a runway model. Before my mother was born, nonna—Italian for grandmother—had been a concert pianist with the Syracuse Symphony Orchestra.

"Let's read some Dante together," she said to me one day. "Of all the Italian poets, he's my favorite. Everyone knows the opening lines of the *Inferno,* about his being in the middle of his journey through life." She paused for a moment and then began to recite, "*Nel mezzo del cammin di nostra vita.*" Her vowels were open and pure and lightly stressed, making the words sound like music. Clearly, she hadn't forgotten anything from her early days in Rome.

"Although I love the *Inferno,*" she said gently rolling the "r", "my favorite Dante is the sonnet about his young muse, the beautiful Beatrice. Do you know it?"

This was one of the poems I had learned by heart with Mr. Caselli. It was one of my favorites, too, and it was my chance to show off. "Isn't that the one that goes something like this?" I said and closed my eyes. While dramatically clutching my hand over my heart, I recited, "*Tanto gentile e tanto onesta...*" so gentle and so pure, in a slow, deliberate cadence. It was magic: such was the joy.

As I stood at the rail of the *Cristoforo Colombo* and watched the New York skyline slowly recede, I reflected on the stepping stones that had led me to purchase a ticket and board this ship to Italy.

On the morning of the final day at sea, the ship landed in Genoa, where I took a train to the medieval city of Siena in southern Tuscany. I stayed in Siena for a month with Lauro's younger sister, Elena, and her family in a villa just outside of town. This gave me a chance to learn more about Lauro and hear firsthand what he was like growing up. "From an early age, he was a restless dreamer," his sister said. "And I remember he loved to read Dante out loud at the dinner table."

After Siena, I traveled to Rome, where I spent seven months living with Roberto Vacca, Lauro's nephew, and his wife, Stefania, who lived in a rooftop apartment that overlooked St. Peter's Basilica. Roberto was too young to remember much about his uncle. However, the apartment was within easy walking distance of the Janiculum, one of the Seven Hills of Rome. The Janiculum was where the Italian government had placed the famous bust of Lauro deBosis alongside the other heroes of the nation's history. Often, on afternoons when I wasn't busy with my studies at the University of Rome or out with friends, I'd climb to the top of the Janiculum to read Dante's poetry while resting against the statue of Lauro deBosis.

Standing next to the bust of Lauro deBosis in Rome. The statue was defaced by neo-Fascists. June 1985.

Becoming a Physician

Chapter Four:
Give 'Em Hell!

"I've decided I want to become a physician," I told my academic advisor, Melvin Whitmore, in February 1956, during my sophomore year at Haverford College outside of Philadelphia. We were sitting in his office in the science building. "And I'm going to major in English literature," I added.

This second declaration seemed to surprise and disappoint Professor Whitmore. I'd received the top grade in his inorganic chemistry course freshman year, and I believe he'd hoped I'd major in chemistry. The truth was that I had no special love or gift for the subject; I'd simply had a superb course in chemistry during my last year in high school that had covered much of the same material.

"Since I'll get plenty of science in med school," I continued, "I plan on taking only the minimum pre-med requirements."

Most medical schools required only four undergraduate science courses, though more were strongly recommended. To improve their chances of being admitted to medical school, pre-med students typically majored in one of the sciences and sought out extracurricular activities that would make their applications more attractive. It was a perfectly reasonable course of action to gain entrance into a highly competitive and prestigious profession. But to my mind, there would be plenty of science in medical school. I was determined to use college to obtain the best possible liberal arts education.

"I won't say you're crazy," my advisor said. "But without a strong science background, you flat-out won't be competitive." Whitmore had a well-known flair for the dramatic. After a brief pause, he glanced at my arm and added, "You don't want any more strikes against you than you can help." I suddenly felt humiliated and disgraced. Why was I confiding in him? I didn't even like him. Since my bout with polio, I had lost twenty pounds and my right arm was permanently paralyzed. I was still struggling with my altered body image. Whitmore turned in his chair to look out the window. "Medical schools might not even consider your application if they know about your, ah, condition." He was unable to say the word "paralysis," or even meet my eye.

I believed that he was right. This was decades before the Americans with Disabilities Act, and discrimination against the disabled was still perfectly legal. Perhaps I was crazy to think I could get into medical school without more science and a healthy body. Nevertheless, his reaction stunned me. I sat there immobile, barely breathing, until I became lightheaded and my useless right hand began to tingle.

"I've talked to Dean Cadbury," I said finally, taking a deep breath, "and he says if I can keep my grades up he'll be willing to write a letter of recommendation." Dean Cadbury was the advisor for pre-med students. Without his support, getting into medical school would be virtually impossible. "Cadbury thinks there's a trend for schools to accept students with broader backgrounds. He believes this will help my chances."

There were other aspects to my college record that I thought might work in my favor. Although my freshman grades had been above average, I'd excelled in other areas. I'd played trombone in the Bryn Mawr-Haverford student orchestra and in a college jazz ensemble, and at the end of the year had been elected president of the orchestra for the following term. I'd written for the school newspaper and had co-written and directed the freshman class play for the annual inter-class competition. During second semester, my class had elected me to the student council. At year's end, I'd been selected by the faculty as the outstanding freshman. I'd thought about attending medical school, but despite that stellar first year, deep down I was still ambivalent about a career in medicine.

"I didn't always want to become a physician," I suddenly admitted to Whitmore in a burst of candor. "I used to think of it as Plan B—if I couldn't come up with something better."

Before my illness, I'd had no idea where I was headed in life. I'd taken three years of French in high school and then another during my freshman year in college along with an introduction to Spanish. I liked languages and had toyed with the idea of pursuing a career in the Foreign Service. At the same time, I had no great desire to major in French.

"Oh, great—medicine as Plan B!" Whitmore said sarcastically. "That's what I always wanted. A physician who couldn't think of something better to do." He was right. But now my attitude had changed. I was no longer a naïve 18-year-old.

"I'm not afraid to admit polio has forced me to make some hard choices," I explained to my advisor. "It may be the only good thing that came out of that whole experience."

Whitmore nodded, but I doubted he had any idea what I was talking about. How could he? Life-threatening illness is such a private, personal experience. It can tear at your soul and ravage your mind. How can anyone else hope to understand this? And yet, it blessed me with an abiding understanding of the dark nature of illness that's not accessible to most people, much less the typical physician. Polio also taught me about the fragility of existence in the full flower of youth and how disease can corrupt everything. These were lessons that, ironically, were to enrich my life and empower my talents as a physician.

Although few people I encountered had shared my experience, when I finally applied to medical school, I believe I was able to communicate the lessons I'd learned to interviewers. I didn't consciously think of using my illness as a strategy, but in the end, ironically, the "strike against me" which my advisor couldn't even bring himself to name, may have helped me to get accepted.

*****

During spring break, a few weeks after my meeting with Whitmore, my parents urged me to meet with Dr. Max Wexler, a physician with a disability whom they'd met in their church. "I'm sure you'll make a fine physician," Wexler pronounced, from his manual wheelchair next to the fireplace in his living room. "I can see by the way you use your hands that you won't have any difficulty in medical school," he added, apparently not noticing that I didn't actually have "hands"—as my paralyzed right hand lay motionless in my pants pocket. His baseless optimism left me thoroughly depressed, and seeing him in his wheelchair brought flashbacks of being trapped in the wooden respirator in Madrid. For several nights after our meeting, I'd wake up in the middle of the night gasping for air. *What's my body trying to tell me?* I wondered.

"Despite what Dr. Wexler says, I don't think medicine's for me," I told my parents. "I wouldn't go to that jerk in a million years. Who would ever want a disabled physician?" I had the same prejudices everyone else had about disability: they aren't whole, they can't do, they aren't competent. In a word, they're inferior.

A short time later, however, I had a far more encouraging encounter with another physician, Dr. Howard Rusk, whom I met through friends of my parents. Rusk was the Chairman of the Department of Rehabilitation Medicine at New York University's School of Medicine and is considered the father of modern rehabilitation medicine. He was one of the first to champion specialized rehabilitation services to help wounded World War II veterans return to their communities. I trusted him to tell me the truth about the practicality of pursuing a career in medicine.

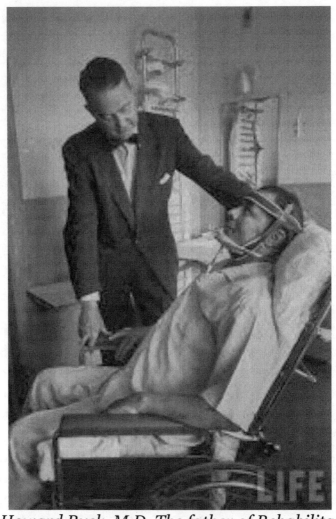

Howard Rusk, M.D. The father of Rehabilitation Medicine in the U.S. with an injured patient.

In his office, surrounded by pictures of him shaking hands with presidents, generals and dignitaries from around the world, I recounted my experience with polio. He didn't say much but was clearly interested in my story.

"I'm back at school fulltime, my general health is excellent and I'd like to study medicine. But if medical schools won't accept me because of my disability, I need to make other plans. What do you think?"

Without hesitating, he stood up, leaned over his desk to shake my hand and gave me a broad smile. "I think," he said, "you should give 'em hell!"

Give 'em hell! What a beautiful thing to say. That was the message I needed to hear. I almost danced out of his office.

With his words ringing in my ears, I decided I needed to raise the issue of my disability head-on with key decision-makers at several medical schools. I called the admissions office at Harvard Medical School and explained my situation to the secretary, who recommended that I talk directly to the Dean, Dr. George Berry.

Encouraged, I traveled to Boston, but as I climbed the steps outside the administration building, I was overwhelmed with anxiety. I wasn't even applying to med school yet. The Dean would think me a fool for wasting his time.

I needn't have worried. It was early June and the summer recess had already begun. Dr. Berry was relaxed and talkative. Our conversation lasted well over an hour, nearly twice the time allotted.

"If my grades are the same as another candidate's without a disability, would I be turned down?" I asked Berry. I didn't realize it at the time, but this was something of a trick question. I wasn't applying then. Maybe never. My question was purely hypothetical. How could he possibly be anything but supportive?

"We would never discriminate like that," he said, as if I had just insulted the integrity of Harvard itself. "You come from a great school. If your grades are good, we'd accept you flat-out. No questions asked." Maybe he meant it, maybe he didn't. This was 30 years before anyone had heard of disability rights. Regardless, I spent the rest of that warm June day wandering around the medical school campus breathing in the intoxicating air of fresh possibilities.

Following my interview, I sent Berry a letter thanking him for his time and making sure to put in writing that my disability would not be a disqualification for entering Harvard. In fact, I wasn't particularly interested in Harvard, but I figured if they'd say "yes," perhaps other schools would have the same attitude.

In the fall of 1956, I made an appointment with Dr. Leonard Fenninger, Dean of the Medical School at the University of Rochester in upstate New York. Rochester was my first choice, as a number of friends from college had praised the small classes and excellent faculty.

I asked Dean Fenninger the same question I'd posed to Dean Berry. By then, I was already taking classes towards my major in English literature and was studying Italian with the idea of spending a year in Italy after college. I also asked Dr. Fenninger if taking the minimum pre-med courses would disqualify my candidacy.

"Of course not," he said, although we both knew that the vast majority of accepted students pile on as many pre-med courses as possible, many even taking more in summer school. "We want students who are, above all, well-rounded." This encouraged me to ask the next question.

"If I took a year off between college and medical school to study abroad, would that hurt my chances of being accepted?"

"Absolutely not," he replied. "I wish I had done that." I wasn't sure I believed him, but it was what I wanted to hear.

"Even if I were to, say," I hesitated, "spend the year in Rome studying Italian literature?"

"What a great idea," he said. "That would be wonderful."

Wow, I thought. Did he really say it would be wonderful if I took a year off to study in Rome? And at that moment, I knew it was exactly what I was going to do.

It's important to emphasize this conversation was 100 percent hypothetical, though it had the advantage of making him sound like a very fair and open-minded individual. After all, doesn't everybody want a doctor who is well-rounded? Versed in the liberal arts? The interview couldn't have gone better if I'd scripted it myself. I promptly wrote Dr. Fenninger a letter thanking him for his encouragement and sound advice about my pre-med courses and studying abroad.

Later, however, as I reflected on my visit to Rochester, I worried that I'd been duped. "I think the Dean was feeling sorry for me," I told my mother. "They're not going to want some student taking up valuable space who can't do surgery or deliver a baby on his own. Why should I even apply?"

"Give yourself more time to think about it," my mother said. Her counsel was always reassuring but she had to admit she had never heard me sound so discouraged. "Remember what Dean Cadbury told you," she added. He was the pre-med advisor at Haverford who had helped countless students get into medical school. "Didn't he say he would write a strong letter of recommendation for you? He wouldn't do that if he didn't think you were a good candidate." She paused and then added, "Wasn't he the one who said college is the time to try your wings?"

Despite my apprehension that no medical school would accept me, I had to entertain the possibility that Dean Fenninger had meant what he said. I made two more trips to Rochester to sit in on a few classes and, afterwards, talk with the professors. These visits also gave me a chance to strike up a friendship with the staff in the dean's office and, in particular, with his personal secretary, Harriet Purdy, who began to take a special interest in my candidacy. In this way, I developed a first name relationship with key players and became a face and someone with a specific identity rather than just one more number in an admissions office flooded with applications.

In early October 1958, I sailed to Italy for my year of study abroad. By this time I'd applied to med school at Columbia University and Case Western University in Cleveland as well as Rochester. I figured my acceptance was in the hands of the gods. "I need to have fun, learn some Italian and make the most of my time abroad," I told myself as I stood at the ship's rail and watched the New York skyline slowly disappear. "This is the adventure of a lifetime."

In late February 1959, while I was living in Rome and attending classes at the University of Rome, I received a letter from Rochester. "Congratulations!" it began. "This is to inform you that you have been invited to join the medical school class of 1963."

Much later, I learned from Harriet Purdy

that my application had provoked a contentious debate within the admissions committee. When it was finally put to a vote, I apparently squeaked by with a margin of only a single 'yea'.

But all I knew on that day in Rome was that I'd been accepted. No qualifications, no requirement that I take advanced organic chemistry that summer. Just an acceptance, plain and simple. I was ecstatic. The letter ended with these words: "We have every confidence that you will make an outstanding physician. Welcome to Rochester!"

*****

Four years later, on the eve of my graduation from medical school, my classmates and I sat with our guests and members of the faculty in Whipple auditorium—named for George Whipple, the medical school's first Dean.

"Congratulations," students shouted back and forth to each other. "Never thought I'd make it," others said. Students and their families were shaking hands and clapping each other on the back. The celebratory atmosphere contrasted with the dour portraits of the school's founders on the walls.

"We may be graduating," one classmate said, "but it's really just the beginning. Now the real work starts."

While the University-wide graduation of several thousand students would take place on Sunday afternoon, Friday night in Whipple was reserved for a more intimate ceremony to honor the 72 new physicians in the class of 1963.

The program included speeches from the Dean and several faculty members. Charlie Tobin, a favorite anatomy professor, made an analogy between the med students and caterpillars emerging from the chrysalis stage as butterflies. The chairman of Neurology recalled his grueling years of training as a physician. This was followed by an internist from the community who reflected on the joys and challenges of private practice. In addition to these talks, I was also on the program. Three weeks earlier, I'd been chosen by my classmates to give a commencement address on their behalf. As I sat in the front row waiting for my name to be called, I thought back not to the past four years of study but to the improbable journey that had led to my being accepted into one of the top medical schools in the first place.

Finally, the Dean stepped to the podium. "Now it's my pleasure to introduce the representative of the graduating class of 1963 to give a commencement address," he said. "Please give a warm welcome to Dr. Lauro Halstead."

Amidst the applause, I got up from my seat and stepped to the microphone. As I got ready to read my remarks, I looked out at the audience and realized I had done it. I had done my best to give 'em hell!

Chapter Five:
This Honorable Profession

"Gently lift the fascia with the forceps and separate it away from the underlying layer of muscle," I read aloud to my three fellow medical students. The four of us had been assigned to work as a team in the centuries-old tradition of dissecting a human cadaver. On the first morning of the first day of medical school, I'd been elected to read aloud from the Gross Anatomy textbook as the others took turns with their scalpels. We forced ourselves to ignore the pungent odor of formaldehyde and, instead, concentrate on the unpleasant task at hand.

"It's a trial by fire," the anatomy professor had said. "If you can't handle dissection, you don't belong in medicine." By the end of the third day, two classmates out of a class of seventy-four had told the Dean that they'd had enough.

Fortunately, our team of four survived the first week huddled around a desiccated old woman who'd donated her body so we could learn about her nerves and muscles and bones.

"Let's call her Molly," one of my cadaver mates suggested.

"No way," said another. "That's my grandmother's name. How about Gertie? After my ex-girlfriend."

So we called our cadaver Gertie, or Gertie Girl, even though we couldn't see her face. Cadavers are always laid out prone so the first part of the body students dissect is the back. Later, during the second month, the cadaver is turned over so you can dissect the face, which is the most physically and emotionally challenging part of the body.

"Next identify the infraspinatus muscle," I read. The formaldehyde, which permeated the air with the smell of death, forced me to turn my back to Gertie Girl. By keeping my eyes focused on the textbook, I could avoid looking at her pale, lifeless flesh. We decided that Gertie Girl had been a virgin and must've been close to seventy when she died.

"This muscle attaches medially to the infraspinous fossa of the scapula and laterally to the middle facet of the greater tubercle of the humerus." I struggled to translate this passage into English for the other members of the team. "I think it means the infraspinatus muscle goes from the inner border of the scapula or shoulder blade all the way over to the upper arm bone."

My translation provoked a raucous uproar. "Way to go, Lauro," one of my classmates shouted as he waved a scalpel in the air. "Your year in Italy is going to come in real handy." My three colleagues, all biology majors (two had even done postgrad research), had seemed a bit dumbfounded when I'd proudly told them I'd spent the past year studying Italian literature in Rome.

But it turned out that memorizing a lot of Italian vocabulary might not have put me at a disadvantage. Our task now was to memorize as much as we could as fast as possible. Shortly before the Thanksgiving holiday, I was taking a coffee break with Randall, one of my cadaver mates who always had a gracious word of encouragement. He had spent the previous year researching at NIH and was probably the smartest member of our class.

"We're all surprised by how well you seem to be doing," Randall said. "You know—English major, minimum pre-med courses and then a year gallivanting around Italy. "We weren't sure this proud profession was for you."

"I'm a little surprised myself," I said, both pleased and reassured by his praise. "If I can just get through anatomy and biochemistry, I think I'll make it."

I was enthusiastic about my classes because most of what I was learning was completely new to me. It was a kind of voyage of discovery, not just in anatomy but in the other first-year courses such as histology and biochemistry. Learning the names of bones and how they fit together and seeing cellular structures for the first time was unexpectedly enjoyable.

"You're going to laugh," I said to Randall,

"but learning Italian has been surprisingly helpful. Many medical terms have their roots in Latin and, of course, so does Italian. Studying medicine is like learning a new language."

"I've had the same thought," Randall said. "I went on patient rounds the other day up on the surgical ward. I needed a translator because I couldn't make sense of what they were saying."

The big course second semester was physiology, which dealt with how the body works day-to-day as well as in response to stress. I did okay on the pop quizzes, but the big exam just before spring break was a disaster. Four days before the exam, I'd received a letter from my girlfriend, who was in graduate school in New York City. We'd been going together since college and I was on the verge of asking her to marry me.

"This is to let you know I have found someone else," she wrote. "He has asked to marry me and we're going to be married in June."

It was a terrible blow. Six weeks earlier, she'd flown up to Rochester for a Valentine's Day visit. We'd been very close and I'd never doubted her love. Now it was over. I didn't eat. I couldn't sleep. And I certainly didn't study. I managed to show up for the physiology exam, but when confronted with three essay questions, my mind went blank. I sat there staring at the empty sheet of paper. I didn't write a word and failed the test. Suddenly, my whole medical career was in jeopardy.

The Chair of the Department of Physiology, Dr. William Lotspeitch, called me into his office and asked me to explain why I hadn't written a single word in the examination booklet. I told him about my girlfriend's letter, but was too ashamed and too afraid to request a second chance.

"How are you ever going to function as a physician?" Lotspeitch demanded. "Doctors have stress in their lives all the time. There are going to be big disappointments. But you have to rise above that and still do your job."

The next day, the Dean told me that I was on academic probation. One more screw-up and I was out of there.

Fortunately, the following week was spring break. I canceled plans to return home and buried myself in the library. The physiology course was pass/fail. I never learned what my final grade was but, at the end of the term, all that mattered was my transcript said "pass".

My second year of medical school proved to be even more challenging and stressful than my first. Beginning with my senior year in college, I'd had three different orthopedic surgeries on my hands and arms during each school holiday: Thanksgiving, Christmas and Easter. The day after graduation from college, I had a fourth. In all of these major procedures, bones were fused to take the place of useless muscles. This gave me limited control over my paralyzed right arm and hand.

Fortunately, I'd had no surgery during the first year of medical school, but that summer I had a fifth procedure, this time a fusion of the bones in my right wrist. Because of the profound weakness of my right arm, normal blood flow was significantly reduced in that limb, so the surgical incision healed slowly. Instead of closing over in three to four weeks, as would normally be the case, the incision still hadn't healed at the beginning of the fourth month, when I was already back at school with a full load of classes. To protect the wound, I wore a cast which extended from my elbow to my fingertips and carried it in a sling around my neck. The weight of the cast made everyday tasks as well as schoolwork slow and arduous. Shortly before the Christmas break, I started to run a low-grade fever. I returned home early to see my orthopedic surgeon, Dr. Robert Carroll, who worked at Columbia-Presbyterian Hospital in New York City and was a pioneer in upper limb reconstruction.

Carroll saw that I had an infection and wanted to operate as soon as possible, though he wasn't optimistic that a sixth procedure would work. And indeed, nothing went as planned. When I got back to school in early January, a second infection was discovered—

one which turned out to be resistant to all available antibiotics, even to the newest "big guns."

The consultant for infectious diseases at Rochester told me I'd have to either drop out for a semester or go into strict isolation. "This bug is damn dangerous and we can't let it get into the patient wards."

"If I go into isolation, how will I stay up with my schoolwork?" I asked. It would be impossible to attend classes from an isolation room.

"You seem to have a penchant for doing things differently," my friend Randall said, when he heard about the isolation ward. For the next six weeks, since I missed all my classes, I only managed to survive through the kindness of Randall and others who made copies of their class notes which the nurses then passed to me.

One evening, about halfway through my confinement, a nurse asked me how my spirits were. Like everyone else who came near me, she wore disposable paper garments from head to foot. I guessed she was close to my age, though all I could see were pretty brown eyes peering from above her face mask.

"I'm going crazy in here," I said, my voice rising in anger. "This is worse than medieval torture. Alone all day. No one dares touch me. I'm losing my mind." I didn't mean it literally, but Brown Eyes didn't know that.

The next day, the Chair of the Department of Psychiatry, Dr. John Romano, paid me a visit. He was a tall, imposing man who had an international reputation as an educator and scholar. To my amazement, he wore no protective garments and simply stood in the corner, twirling his face mask around his finger while we talked. At last he said, "Hang in there, Lauro. You're tough. You'll be all right."

The days dragged on, but by early March the infection was miraculously gone. I returned to my classes and to a life outside the hospital.

*****

My last two years of medical school—the clinical years, when you begin to treat patients—were easier sailing: no more heartbreak or pesky infections. I loved the clinical rotations: four to eight weeks on the different specialty wards such as pediatrics, neurology and internal medicine. With each rotation came a gradual increase in responsibility and autonomy. Now I knew I'd made the right career choice, although I still wasn't sure which specialty to pursue.

Before medical school, I'd thought psychiatry would be a good fit, for both my temperament and my disability: I'd be able to sit in a comfortable chair all day and talk with patients. But despite my affection for Dr. Romano, I was disillusioned to discover that psychiatry was still in its infancy—more about theories than about searching for a chemical basis of mental illness. The field seemed stagnant in contrast to other areas of medicine. So I decided to do specialty training in internal medicine which meant learning manual skills such as drawing blood and starting IVs as well as more complex tasks such as performing lumbar punctures and bone marrow aspirations. This was no small consideration with my impaired right arm and hand.

One middle-aged patient, Mr. Stanton, who'd been assigned to me during my third year rotation on the internal medicine service, stared at my right arm as I approached him with a small tray full of needles, syringes and bandages. "What are you going to do?" he asked. "How are you going to draw my blood with one hand?" He'd had a heart attack recently and looked like he might have another.

"Trust me," I said, my own heart racing. "I do this all the time." Anxious patients made me nervous, regardless of how good my skills were. I inspected his right arm for promising veins. "I will, however, need your help."

"Need my help?" Mr. Stanton cried. "You must be crazy. I've got a weak heart." It wasn't the first time I'd gotten such a reaction. However, I had discovered that asking patients for help—to get them actively engaged, even in a small way—provided a distraction, helping both of us relax.

"That's right," I said. "If you agree, there are three things I want you to do which will make this easier for both of us." He looked doubtful but I didn't wait for his answer. "First of all, I want you to close your eyes and imagine a peaceful scene, say, lying in the sun on a sandy beach." With his eyes closed, I silently counted to ten as I arranged everything I would need close to his arm, including several cotton balls and bandages. "Next, take three really deep breaths and exhale slowly." I could see the lines in his face relax as his chest rose and fell. While he was distracted, I put a tourniquet in place and quickly inserted a needle into his vein. The surgery on my right hand had provided me with just enough strength to hold the barrel of the syringe while I pulled back on the plunger with my left hand. "Finally," I said, when the syringe was full, "I want you to open your eyes and take that cotton ball lying next to your arm." He opened his eyes and looked at me, surprised. "Now, as I remove the needle, place the cotton on your arm and press down." It was over in seconds.

"How in the world did you do that, doc?" Mr. Stanton asked. "I didn't feel a thing."

Not all patients were as cooperative as Mr. Stanton and, occasionally, there was someone who absolutely refused to let me do anything. But that happened to other medical students as well.

"Who taught you how to do IVs?" the head nurse on 3-C asked, giving me a quick smile. It was toward the end of my fourth-year rotation on the surgical unit. "I don't know if anyone ever told you," she continued, "but if our nurses have a hard time getting an IV started, I tell them to call you." It was the ultimate compliment: rescuing the experts.

"I learned mostly from you nurses and a few friendly interns, to tell you the truth," I said. In those days, most hospitals didn't have special teams of phlebotomists or persons who draw blood. "But for me," I told her, "the real trick was taking a procedure normally done with two hands and reimagining it, step-by-step, being done with one hand."

Actually, the fingers on my right hand had just enough strength to provide a little help. For tasks like holding a bottle of IV fluid, I used my knees. But when someone has two good hands, there is no need to think creatively.

*****

In May 1963, about a month before graduation, my classmates nominated me to give a valedictory speech during an evening ceremony held at the medical school. This was an unanticipated honor. I was not a standout student, although I did contribute to a number of class activities: first year, I co-founded and co-edited a student journal; fourth year, I helped organize a class musical revue in which I also sang several numbers; I was also co-editor and wrote the text for the class yearbook.

The commencement speech provided an unexpected opportunity to reflect on recent advances as well as several disturbing trends in current medical practice, some of which had been present for many years.

Throughout history, physicians have been highly esteemed, even when the cure was sometimes worse than the disease. Alchemists and barber surgeons had prestigious callings and were paid for their services. When doctors were finally able to perform painless surgery and cure infectious diseases, the medical profession became even more revered, with some even thinking about physicians as gods. It is a precious mantel to inherit, and there is little wonder that medical schools are flooded with applications. In recent years, however, despite advances such as robotic surgery and genomic medicine, the medical profession has been tarnished in this country. Some doctors have become motivated by greed and have learned to equate success with income, rather than with medical skill or patient satisfaction. There is no simple explanation for this phenomenon; medicine, like other professions, is a reflection of the culture. Capitalism and market forces have sometimes trumped traditional physicians' ethics that date back centuries. Although discussions of these issues weren't part of the curriculum during my four years of medical school, they were clearly on my mind.

My graduation speech, entitled *This Honorable Profession* was written more than fifty years ago, but was amazingly prescient regarding American medicine in the 21st century.

I began with a discussion of how modern technology was leading to an impersonalization of medical care.

"...medical practice has changed in several fundamental ways over the past few decades as a result of our increased scientific and technical knowledge. Perhaps the major change has been a subtle shift in emphasis from the physician and his art to his tools... A byproduct of this increased emphasis on the physician's tools has been a gradual impersonalization of medical care... While patients are happy with being cured of more illnesses, they are increasingly dissatisfied with the manner in which it is accomplished... patients don't understand why doctors have to be different from what they were years ago to offer competent healthcare. What the public seems to want is a combination of both worlds—an old-

fashioned doctor who can offer modern medicine."

I then discussed how better diagnostic tests and more sophisticated treatment options inevitably lead to increased costs. This dynamic, fifty years later, has resulted in popular and well-reimbursed specialties and subspecialties that fund expensive procedures over careful attention to a patient's medical history and physical exam. This has given rise to an upward spiral of ever more expensive care.

This led to the next topic which was the impact of money on medicine.

"... Medicine and money have never mixed particularly well. The doctor makes his money from other people's pain and is obliged to render a bill whether he is successful or not. Since there are always sick people, doctors rarely starve, and to the contrary, now that medical costs are so high, doctors are often quite rich. In fact, in many people's minds, the doctor has become the symbol of the rich, fat, satisfied citizen. It's a curious situation that young people who are motivated by a sense of service and dedication should come to be identified with the pursuit of the almighty dollar... It reflects the sad fact that many doctors are greedy for the fast buck. Fee splitting, padded bills and unnecessary operations justify the image of a rich man who can afford to be sued."

Even the most cynical among my medical

school classmates of 1963 could not have anticipated the level of greed and corruption uncovered in a recent Medicare investigation, in
which auditors found that some doctors had
billed the government for more than $50 mil-
lion in a single year.

I also mentioned that specialization was
leading to a fragmentation of healthcare, with
each practitioner doing a smaller fraction of
the whole. My prediction was that this was
turning *"...the practice of medicine more and
more into an eight-hour job."*

This is not to say that the vast majority of
doctors don't work hard or provide honorable,
honest services to their patients. But the disturbing trend lines were already visible back in
the early 1960's. Today, more and more physicians are choosing specialties that promise
fixed hours, such as that of the hospitalist, who
is generally an internist working eight-hour
hospital shifts taking care of other doctors' patients.

Finally, I chastised the American Medical
Association for not doing a better job of polic-
ing its members and not always championing
the public good. In particular, I cited the
AMA's history as a powerful Washington lobby
which worked hard to block the creation of national health insurance.

My intention with this speech was to be
thoughtful and reflective; I did not intend to

hurt anyone's feelings, especially considering the many gifts that Rochester had given me. Unfortunately, I didn't know that the new Dean of the medical school, Dr. Donald Anderson, who was the master of ceremonies that night, was also a former president of the AMA.

What I'd said about the AMA was true, but Dr. Anderson heard it as a personal attack on him as well as on the entire medical profession. The consequences were almost disastrous.

When I finished, an eerie silence settled over the auditorium. Had the microphone been turned off? Why did everyone look stunned? Then, starting in the back and rippling slowly toward the front, wave upon wave of joyous, even raucous applause washed over me. There were shouts of "Hear, hear," and even a few whistles. My classmates may have loved it, but Dr. Anderson, whom I hadn't met previously, was offended. During my talk, I later heard, he'd grabbed his chest and bent forward as though having a coronary.

I gave this speech on the Friday night before the formal, University-wide commencement ceremony the following Sunday. I later learned that the Dean was so angry he made a brief attempt to block my graduation. But as we now know, many of the concerns about my treasured profession that I raised on that June evening are even more pertinent today.

One of my career regrets is that I didn't play

a more active role in addressing these issues. However, I'm not temperamentally inclined to rock the boat—at least not enough for sustained activism. I was also keenly aware of the price my father had paid—and the jobs he'd lost—because he'd spoken out about perceived unfairness or injustices in environments where he worked. Such passion wasn't in my makeup.

Although the Dean might not have believed it, my words that evening were spoken out of a deep respect and love for this honorable profession which has blessed me with countless opportunities to fulfill myself beyond all expectation.

Medical Career

Chapter Six:
Rolling Stone

"What's my problem?" I shouted into the dark. I was lying in a motel bed next to a twenty-one-year-old German au pair I had been dating for about six months. It was December 1970 and we were staying at a Motel 6 in Saginaw, Michigan, a failing industrial city notable for its vacant lots littered with the rusted hulks of abandoned cars.

I quickly lowered my voice so as not to wake my companion as I continued my conversation with the dark. "It's 2 a.m. and I need sleep."

She was a young woman from a blue-collar family in Munich who was hanging out with a divorced physician from Rochester, New York. I didn't know German and she was still struggling with English. The only language we really had in common was sex.

My head was throbbing with booze and drugs. "I need another 10 of Valium."

Grasping onto a chair, I stood up and stumbled into the bathroom. In the morning, I had an appointment for a job interview as director of a community outreach program associated with the medical school at Michigan State University. I wasn't interested in the position but as a medical colleague advised, "To keep your job at home, look for work elsewhere." The trouble was my job at "home" in Rochester was going nowhere.

A few years earlier, everyone I knew had been jealous of my good fortune. I'd graduated in 1963, six months before President Kennedy's assassination, and was promptly caught up in the early draft for the Vietnam War. Physicians were urgently needed to treat wounded young American soldiers on the battlefield. Because of my polio disability, I readily flunked the Army physical but in 1965, as part of my four years' post-medical school specialty training in internal medicine, I got assigned to another kind of battlefield in the emergency room of a large city hospital in Washington, D.C. Night after night we treated young and old alike for drug overdoses, stabbings and gunshot wounds. Most patients had no health insurance and many were living on the streets. This was the same country that was preparing to send men to the moon.

Toward the last year of my postgraduate training in internal medicine, I received a phone call from Rochester inviting me to be the director of a program in international medicine. The job would involve taking medical students overseas during the summer months to study exotic diseases. Since I loved travel and foreign languages, it sounded ideal.

The reality was far less glamorous. Since I

had no staff and a small budget, I had to organize every trip down to the last detail. In addition, it was my job to raise the money to cover the travel expenses for myself and the six to eight medical students who joined me. I managed to perform this high-wire act for two summers, traveling each year to a remote Andean city in Colombia, South America. Together with host students and faculty, we carried out epidemiological studies of local diseases. It was exhausting work, and while the students loved it, I was out of my depth: I spoke limited Spanish, I had no experience in cross-cultural research nor any training in epidemiology. When I closed the program after the second year, no one at the medical school said a word.

In addition to these South American trips, I was expected to carry a full load of academic duties: committees, teaching, research and patient care. None of it seemed to suit my temperament or play to my strengths. But what *were* my strengths? Part of my problem was that I didn't know myself well enough to answer that question. Therefore, I did what any sane person would do in my position: I started to drink. And take drugs.

Now I was in Saginaw, Michigan, three years after having moved to Rochester, pretending to look at a job I didn't want. I went into the bathroom and splashed cold water on my face. Gazing at my reflection in the mirror,

I hardly recognized the haggard person staring back at me: slightly thinning blond hair, dark circles that emphasized the grey in my blue eyes, hollow cheeks from eating too much junk food. How had I fallen so far? I rinsed out a Styrofoam cup and half filled it with Johnny Walker Black Label. The taste made me nauseous. *I don't know why I drink this crap,* I thought, as I washed down another 10 mg. pill of Valium. I hated the taste, and in the morning I'd be hung over.

I lay down on the bed and covered my head with a thin pillow that smelled of cigarettes. "Oh, *scheisse!*" The word for shit was one of the few German words I'd learned from Miss Munich, a pet name I'd given my girlfriend.

I hated the smell of tobacco. She rolled over, half awake, half naked. The combination of alcohol, Valium and stale cigarette smoke made the room spin. I sat up and turned on a small table lamp.

In the half light, I staggered over to the window next to the bed. It had begun snowing, and a fierce north wind was driving a mix of snow and hail hard against the glass. The scratching sound was like someone trying to get in. Or out. Across from the motel, a lone streetlight left most of a vast parking lot of used cars in shadow. It made for a desolate view. "Sag-i-naw!" I said to myself. Even the name sounded depressing. It was a perfect metaphor for the dark night of my soul.

"*Scheisse!*" Miss Munich said as she sat up, covering her nakedness. She stared at me with pale blue eyes. How could this Nordic creature be so beautiful in the dead of night? "Vat's ze matter?" she whispered. Her German accent made the question sound sexy.

"I can't sleep," I said. "And now my head's spinning and I feel like vomiting." She kissed me on the cheek and then leaned her head on my shoulder. We sat there for a moment in silence. It had been more than a year since I had been using Valium to calm my nerves and drinking at night to help me sleep. "I'm lost," I said finally. "I'm lost and at a dead end."

In the morning, I overslept and was half an hour late for the job interview, though, as it turned out, the physician who was going to interview me had missed his flight from Detroit. There never was a job offer. Saginaw had ended before it began.

Later that afternoon, as we were driving back to Rochester, one of Bob Dylan's songs came on the radio. *How does it feel?* he sang. *How does it feel?* And finally, in words I felt I could have written myself: *To be without a home. Like a complete unknown. Like a rolling stone.*

*****

Back in upstate New York, things were as bleak as ever. Rochester is famous for its grey skies and endless winters. January set a record for most snow days and February was notable for the most days without sunshine. On one of those cold, cheerless days, Miss Munich and I got into an argument that lasted most of the night. In the morning, she was gone and I never saw her again. Now, more than ever, scotch was my best friend.

Since the international program had ended, I'd been working for more than a year on the rehabilitation service of the main teaching hospital. The rehab unit treated patients with chronic physical disabilities that few physicians wanted to deal with: older stroke victims, kids with head injuries and teenagers with spinal cord injuries. Our job was to help people recover their strength and teach them how to cope with new limitations.

As important as working on the rehab unit was, I found it emotionally challenging because it reminded me of my bout with polio and my paralyzed right arm. During medical school and four years of postgraduate training, I'd avoided other polio survivors and patients with disabilities. I, too, had adopted society's stereotypes and saw the disabled as morally weak, incompetent, even unclean. Why would I want to work with them?

Patients in wheelchairs were especially demoralizing: people stuck in ugly, shiny metal contraptions with uncomfortable leg rests and rigid backs. I'd been in one of those wheelchairs for over six months. Although I'd eventually been able to walk again, wheelchairs still symbolized futility, despair, even death. Who would want to be a part of that? Then there was the hard, unyielding fact of paralysis: cold, lonely, useless limbs. I knew all about that each time I caught sight of my right arm dangling by my side. Or perhaps it was simply the patients themselves: helpless, even hopeless. At some level, I was afraid I might become one of them.

Now, however, I was an impaired attending physician taking care of 12 to 15 disabled patients at a time. This meant I spent a lot of time on the unit talking with patients and watching them as they struggled to recover their strength and dignity.

One of them was Peter Stein, an intense, 52-year-old accountant with a history of high blood pressure and diabetes. He'd recently had a stroke.

"Doc, I don't know what's wrong with me," he confided, late one afternoon as I was making bedside rounds with Mrs. Ramsey, the head nurse on the rehabilitation unit. He was lying flat in bed with a sheet covering his partially paralyzed left side. "I feel pretty good in the morning and then as the day goes along, I just run out of gas."

I'd heard this complaint many times from other patients. It was understandable, considering the energy it took to recover from serious illnesses.

I turned to Mrs. Ramsey. "Running out of gas," I repeated. "This is what a lot of patients say." I sat on the edge of the bed. I was in no hurry. I wanted him to think carefully about what I was going to ask.

"Mr. Stein, can you be more specific? Take today. Can you give me an example of running out of gas?"

"Sure, Doc," he replied without hesitating. "I dressed myself this morning and then transferred from the bed to the wheelchair. All without anyone helping me. It was the first time I did it alone. I was so pleased I called my wife to tell her." He brought his right hand up to his face and covered his eyes. He was sobbing. Emotional lability is common following a stroke.

I reached out to hold his paralyzed left hand. "Take your time, Mr. Stein. I've got all day."

After a moment, he looked up. "Then, this afternoon I was so exhausted I couldn't transfer myself from the wheelchair back to the bed. One of the orderlies had to help me. I was ashamed."

It occurred to me that I didn't really understand what Mr. Stein—or any other patient, for that matter—actually did during a 24-hour day. Nor Nurse Ramsey or anyone else on the rehab team. Everyone was too busy treating multiple patients to observe one closely for a full day.

"What's Mr. Stein's Barthel score?" I asked Mrs. Ramsey, referring to the Barthel Index, which measures patient abilities during a rehabilitation program. A higher score meant greater independence in basic living activities such as eating, dressing and bathing.

"His Barthel is 14 out of a possible 20," Mrs. Ramsey replied. "That's pretty good and up from a score of only 9 three weeks ago."

The goal of rehabilitation was to help patients improve their Barthel scores to the point where they were as self-sufficient as possible once they went home. I was beginning to realize, however, that Barthel provided only a crude estimate of a patient's performance. And it certainly didn't reveal when patients like Mr. Stein "ran out of gas".

"You're right," I said. "14 is a pretty good score. But it's misleading. It doesn't tell us *when* Mr. Stein gets exhausted and *what* specific activities require help. That's important information that's completely missing."

I turned to face Mr. Stein. "Could I ask you to help me with a little experiment?" I had just had a flash of insight.

"I want to get a better idea of exactly what happened today," I explained. I drew a long horizontal line on a clean sheet of paper representing a 24-hour period from 7 a.m. to 7 a.m. the following day. "Now, sir, what time did you wake up?" I made a mark on the line to indicate the time he mentioned. Then I walked him through his day, noting what he did, when he did it and whether he needed help. So, for example, he ate breakfast at 8 a.m. by himself and then at 8:30 got dressed and into his wheelchair on his own. It was only later in the day, about 3:30 p.m., that he "ran out of gas" and needed help going to the bathroom and getting back in bed.

By making brief notations on the sheet of paper, I was able to produce a vivid, graphic picture of Mr. Stein's day. I showed the graph to Nurse Ramsey and then Mr. Stein.

"Dr. Halstead," Mrs. Ramsey said. "This is brilliant! I think you're onto something here."

"I agree," Mr. Stein said. "It shows me what I need to work on. I have to do a better job of pacing myself and save my energy for later in the day."

Seeing their enthusiasm, I realized that this simple technique of documenting a patient's behavior could represent a whole new approach to assessing independence. Might it even replace the Barthel Index? It was a question worth pursuing.

Like most ideas, however, the only way to discover if it was practical and useful was to evaluate it in a formal study. I would need to do research. And research, I saw even then, could lead to a compelling new mission—one that, at the age of 35, might fully engage my emotional and intellectual energies and help me resolve the conflict I was experiencing between my roles as healer and impaired self and my patients with disabilities.

Initially, placing patients in the context of a research study created a kind of intellectual wall. It protected me from getting too close to my own disquieting emotions. Only later did the wall start to crumble allowing me to see my patients, and myself, in all our shared vulnerability and fragile humanity.

*****

Slowly, over the next few weeks as I began to write my first research grant, the nightmare of Saginaw began to recede, along with my need for booze and Valium. Research was my new source of comfort and stimulation. Dylan could ask once again, *How does it feel?* And this time I could answer, "Pretty damn good, Bob."

On the way to a fresh start in Houston. June 1973.

The spring of 1971 was the beginning of a long journey of reinvention and discovery in the field of rehabilitation medicine that I would pursue for the next four decades. One question inevitably led to another, and then another, in an endless succession. It was the beginning of a career shift that, based on several publications, would take me within two years to one of the premier rehabilitation hospitals in the country, in Houston, Texas—the ideal home for a rolling stone.

Chapter Seven:
The Best of Both Worlds

Spinal cord injury is an uncommon but devastating condition. Since injured soldiers during the World Wars rarely survived more than one year, it was generally believed that a spinal cord injury was a hopeless condition. In addition to paralysis, these patients lose normal control of blood pressure and temperature and there is altered function of many internal organs. This bleak outlook began to improve during the Vietnam War with advances in battlefield medicine, which in turn stimulated better care in civilian hospitals.

In the early 1970's, the federal government funded several specialized units dedicated to the comprehensive management of spinal injury patients. One of these units was at The Institute for Rehabilitation and Research (TIRR) a teaching hospital in Houston where I was hired in 1973. Although I had little experience treating such patients, I liked the challenge and was eager to learn. Because the injuries were poorly understood, there were many mysteries to solve; this put me and my fellow researchers on the cutting edge of this new field of inquiry. The combination of patient care and clinical research was the best of both worlds and, for the first time in my professional life, my heart and mind were fully engaged.

*****

"Don't hit me!" A young man screamed from inside one of the patient rooms on the spinal cord injury service. "Please. Stop hitting me! I'm completely paralyzed!"

I rushed down the hospital corridor toward the cries. It was the middle of July 1973 and three weeks into my new job as an attending physician at TIRR. I wasn't sure how life would work out in this sprawling southern city, but I had no regrets about leaving the Snow Belt in upstate New York and a job at the medical school where I had struggled for six years to find my place. Making the most of the warm climate, my wife, Kris, and I had bought a comfortable ranch home with a small backyard pool.

"What's going on?" I asked as I entered the room of my teenaged patient, Travis Johnson, who lay stretched out in a corner bed, naked and helpless. He'd sustained a catastrophic neck injury while diving half-drunk into the shallow end of a swimming pool during his 18th birthday party. Damage to his spinal cord resulted in total paralysis of his arms and legs. He was unable to scratch his nose or wiggle a finger, and now he looked frightened.

"He called me a fat nigger," said the nurse's aide, Maylene Bullard, glaring down at Johnson. There were dark patches of sweat under her arms and across the front of her blouse. The air-conditioning unit was no match against the Texas heat and did nothing to cool the racial tension in the air.

"She doesn't know how to give an enema," Johnson said. "She doesn't know nothin' about quads." Quadriplegics or quads, who have lost the use of all four limbs, also lose control of their bowels and bladders. It is one of the most disabling and difficult to manage conditions in medicine, especially for nurses and nurse aides who have to lift deadweight patients and clean up after bowel and bladder accidents.

"Okay, okay," I said. "Let me hear both sides. Maylene, you go first." She wiped the perspiration from her forehead with a towel and took a deep breath. She was clearly frustrated and angry.

"Mr. Johnson," she began, showing the deference of a southern black woman to a white person by using his last name. "Mr. Johnson, he don't respect me. I've worked with the likes of him for 10 years. I know my job and he's supposed to have a bowel program before the evening shift come on," she said, referring to the procedure requiring a suppository or enema to help clean out a patient's intestines.

"Travis," I said. "Maylene is right." If she

had been white, I would have used her last name. In a few short weeks of living in the South, I'd already adopted local racial manners. "Travis, you need someone with experience. Along with your arms and legs, your intestines are paralyzed. To get them working again, we need to do a bowel program every other day." Like many physicians, I said 'we' when someone else would do the actual work. All I did was write the order.

"Okay, Travis," I said looking at my patient. "Your turn. Tell me what happened."

"First off, I got a splittin' headache from Hell," he said in a Texas drawl. At 210 pounds, Travis had been a high school football star and king of his West Texas town and now was at the mercy of an African-American woman trying to do a thankless task. It was a perfect setup for a classic black-white confrontation.

"I've never been touched by no nigger before, especially down there." His eyes bulged as he tried to lift his head off the pillow, looking toward his groin. A clear plastic catheter had been placed in his bladder to drain urine and keep the bladder from over-filling. There was no urine in the catheter and the attached collection bag was empty.

"That's enough," I said sharply, inspecting the catheter more closely. It should have been full of urine. "No racial slurs. Now, what happened?"

"First, she punched my stomach and then slapped my face. Now I got a pounding headache."

"Is that true?" I turned toward Maylene. But before she could answer, I heard Travis make a slight grunt in the back of his throat. Then his eyes went blank and he stopped breathing. I pulled out my stethoscope and listened to his heart. It was barely beating at 40 times a minute. When I checked his blood pressure, it was over 200 systolic. It should have been around 100.

"Travis, wake up," I yelled again and again while pinching his cheek. "Travis, God damn it, talk to me." Nothing. No reaction to pain. No breath. No sign of life. *He's got AD and probably stroked*, I thought. AD or autonomic dysreflexia is one of the most feared complications of quadriplegic patients. Because of injury to the spinal cord, the brain can't do its job to regulate nerve impulses from organs like the bladder or intestines, impulses that cause the blood pressure to go through the roof and the heart to slow towards zero. The most common cause in someone like Travis was a blocked catheter. Without fast action, patients could suffer strokes or even die.

"Quick, Maylene, call the nurse's station," I instructed, trying to keep my voice even as I felt my fear rising. I had read about AD but never had to handle it on my own. Now I was panicking. "It's a code blue. And get one of the nurses in here. STAT!"

During my years of training, I had worked in the emergency room on several rotations. I had loved the hustle and bustle and the need to make snap diagnostic and treatment decisions. But I'd always had someone looking over my shoulder, making the tough calls and giving the right orders. Now I was alone and unsure what to do next.

"His catheter might be blocked," Maylene said calmly. Without hesitating, she took a large syringe from the bedside cabinet and filled it with saline. She handed me the syringe. "I'm not allowed to do it. See if you can unclog the catheter." She flashed me a smile. Her poise helped me think what to do next. Over each patient's bed there were two valves, one for suction and one for oxygen.

"I'll flush the catheter," I said. "Check his airway and then put that mask over his face. Start him on oxygen. Five liters." It had already been several minutes since Travis had taken a breath. Should I start CPR or work on his catheter? I hesitated for an instant and then climbed on his bed to start giving him artificial respiration.

"ABC," I whispered. "ABC. Keep it simple. You can do this." ABC is the mnemonic you learn in training for medical emergencies: A is for airway, B for breathing, C for cardiac. I must have practiced this in drills dozens of times. I took a deep breath. And then another. My tension began to slip away. His life was in my hands but I knew what to do.

"Mrs. Bullard," I said, using her last name this time as a sign of respect and giving her a nod of approval. "Keep that mask over his face and the oxygen running. He needs all he can get." One... two... three... I pushed down with all my weight on his chest cage at about 60 per minute to give him cardiac compressions. I was about to give him mouth to mouth resuscitation when two nurses came rushing into the room with the medical director of the spinal cord injury service, Dr. Ed Carter. One of the nurses was pushing a crash cart that contained all the medications and equipment used in hospital emergencies. "We've got a serious problem here," I said announcing the obvious. "Travis Johnson. 18 years old with recent high spinal injury. Last blood pressure over 200, heart rate 40. Complained of a pounding headache and then stopped breathing. Maybe three minutes ago, maybe more." I glanced up at the clock on the wall. "He's got AD and I think he stroked." It was 2:25 p.m.

"I'll call the code," Dr. Carter said, indicating that he was now in charge. That was fine with me. I climbed down from the bed and stood back to watch the code team go to work.

Everyone knew their role. "Ms. Parsons, get the Ambu bag," Dr. Carter said as the nurse placed a specialized mask over Travis's face and began pumping air into his lungs. "I'll start the IV. Ms. Friedman, flush out that catheter."

"Halstead," he said, addressing me, "start a flow sheet and record everything we do and when we do it."

We worked on Travis Johnson for more than an hour: IV meds, intubation to suck out secretions from his lungs, even an injection of epinephrine directly into his heart. Eventually, the EKG went flat. He lay cold and motionless. Everyone was exhausted.

"I'm calling it," Dr. Carter finally said. By then, we all knew that this West Texas high school athlete had long been dead. But none of us had wanted to give up.

"Time of death," I pronounced the words carefully, "3:45 p.m."

*****

One week after Travis Johnson died, there was a postmortem conference of the medical and nursing staff to discuss what had happened: had one of the nurses put his catheter in wrong? Had I not acted quickly enough? Could the code blue team have done anything differently? There are always many questions, but no matter how they are answered, they can never bring anyone back.

An autopsy revealed that Johnson had had a congenital blood vessel abnormality in the brain. At some point shortly before I entered the room, the weakened blood vessel, present since birth, had burst due to the high blood pressure. His splitting headache should have tipped me off, but I'd been so focused on trying to be a racial peacemaker that I'd neglected my role as healer. It was a lesson that would haunt me for years.

It was also the first time since my residency that I had come face-to-face with death. One of my patients had died and I had been unable to stop it. I'd stood clueless while he was suffering, his life ebbing away. What kind of physician was I? If our roles had been reversed, and I was stretched out naked on that bed, how would I feel? Would he ever forgive me? Would I ever forgive myself? I couldn't sleep for nights.

*****

At the end of the postmortem conference, Dr. Carter turned to me and shook my hand. "Good work on that case, Halstead." Since he was a recognized expert in the care of spinal cord patients as well as a hard man to please, this was high praise. "Only three weeks on the job and you made all the right calls. I hope you'll stick around." It was exactly what I wanted to hear. Despite the bad outcome, life had to go on, and his vote of confidence helped me to make Houston my home. I stayed in Houston for thirteen very happy and productive years.

In addition to the two worlds of bedside care and clinical research, there was another, less tangible realm that gradually opened up to me during those years. It had to do with personal growth and an increased ease with patients that allowed them to interact with me as a disabled physician. This was especially true later on when I developed new weakness in my legs from polio and had to use a motorized scooter to navigate the long hospital corridors. Despite my apprehension when I'd applied to medical school, my experience with disability, rather than an obstacle, was becoming a powerful asset.

"When did you have your spinal injury?" a young patient asked me once during morning rounds, as he looked at my scooter and paralyzed right arm.

"I had polio in college," I said. "Both polio and spinal injury can cause paralysis, but the paralysis they cause is actually very different." I explained in lay terms that polio is caused by a virus that only damages one type of nerve, while spinal injuries typically damage many nerves. This is why spinal-injured patients are not only paralyzed and without sensation, they also lose control of bowel, bladder and sexual function.

It was in this world that I began to confront my disability more directly and feel more comfortable being open about it, which in turn opened me more to the experiences of others. Did it make me a better physician, a better healer? Perhaps more compassionate? Maybe I had more patience and was able to glimpse for a moment life from someone else's perspective—and see their countless frustrations and disappointments. I've always liked to think I would be the same person in the absence of polio. But how *could* I have been the same? How *could* my medical career have been the same? In the end, we are all shaped by the obstacles we encounter and the ones we have overcome.

Chapter Eight:
It's a Boy!

"Have you seen Ramon?" Valery Michaels, the head nurse, asked me early Monday morning during patient rounds. Ramon Santiago Gutierrez was a well-known jockey who'd injured his spinal cord when a horse fell on him during a race, resulting in paraplegia. He was a Honduran immigrant who had found success on local racetracks and was now my patient at the rehabilitation hospital in Houston. "He went out on a weekend pass Friday evening," Nurse Michaels said, as she examined his medical chart.

It was early spring of 1983, and in those days it was common for patients to leave the hospital for an afternoon or even a whole weekend. Passes away from the hospital were part of the rehabilitation philosophy and designed to ease the transition of seriously ill or injured patients back to their homes. Allowing patients to leave the hospital, however, was a medical responsibility and one I took seriously. If something bad happened to a patient while on pass, the hospital could be sued.

"His wife promised she'd get him back here by now," the nurse said. It wasn't unusual for patients to overstay their passes and come back late. No one likes the idea of being cooped up in the hospital week after week, and getting a patient like Ramon ready for discharge could take two months or more. Although paraplegia is less disabling than quadriplegia, it disrupts many bodily functions and can take years for patients to adjust to the physical and psychological toll. Initial treatment in a rehabilitation hospital is simply the first step in a long journey.

"Didn't Ramon get married fairly recently?" I asked.

"Sometime last fall to Marney Jo Wingate," Nurse Michaels said. "It was a big, fancy wedding that was in all the newspapers. Marney is the daughter of Cornell Wingate, a wealthy Houston businessman."

We were standing next to Ramon's bed. I picked up a framed photograph from a bedside table of a couple on horseback, the man in a tuxedo and the woman in a bridal gown—Mr. and Mrs. Ramon Gutierrez on their wedding day. Attached to the picture was a newspaper article about the joyous occasion. It quoted Ramon bragging about all the children the couple was planning to have.

"Better call Mrs. Gutierrez," I said to Nurse Michaels. "He's at risk for a number of complications if he doesn't get back here soon." The most likely complications were a urinary tract infection and an ulceration of the skin due to a loss in sensation.

Later that morning, we received a phone call from the Houston chief of police. Ramon had been found near a local stable with a bullet in his head. Next to his body, there was a short suicide note in which he apologized to his wife and declared that his life had lost all meaning. Later that week, at his funeral service, his wife tried to explain to me what she thought he meant.

"Ramon was a family-oriented guy," Mrs. Gutierrez said as she wiped away tears with a handkerchief. Her voice was barely audible in the crowd of mourners. "He had five brothers and sisters and wanted a lot of kids of his own." She paused to take a deep breath. "Last weekend...during the pass...you know." The words trailed off as she began sobbing. I took a step closer. "When he discovered that we couldn't do it—" she turned away to hide her face. "He didn't say anything but I knew it was too much for him, you know, the shame. He just wanted so much to have kids."

I gave Mrs. Gutierrez a hug, but I didn't tell her what I was feeling—that her husband's death was my fault. He'd been my patient and my medical responsibility. I'd been the one to sign the order allowing him to leave the hospital. He clearly hadn't been ready to go, and I should have known that. We were good at teaching patients how to deal with the practical aspects of their injuries. But we'd failed to help

Ramon deal with cultural and psychological issues about disability, sexuality and manliness.

For some, adjusting to spinal injury takes a lifetime. Ramon Gutierrez had only had a few weeks. He was a newlywed in a foreign country recovering from a shattering fall. Perhaps it was unrealistic to expect that our team of health professionals—nurses, physical and occupational therapists and a social worker—some of whom were fluent in Spanish—could have prepared someone like Ramon for discharge from the hospital, much less to go out on a weekend pass. And yet, everyone had agreed that he was ready. As the captain of the team, however, I was ultimately responsible for safeguarding his health. I'd let him down, I'd let his wife down, I'd let the whole team down. Life and death. It's a crushing responsibility and I'd failed to fulfill it. What could I possibly say to comfort his grieving widow?

For those of us who worked with spinal injured individuals, the consequences were predictable and they became almost routine. But for each new patient, the injury created a bewildering series of cascading, unpleasant realities that rippled out to virtually every organ and aspect of life.

For both men and women, bowel and bladder function are usually compromised, but in men, who sustain the majority of injuries, there is also an impairment of both erection and ejaculation. With few exceptions, this used to mean that spinal injured men were unable to father children. When I'd taken my job in Houston at a regional spinal cord injury center nearly 10 years earlier, it gave me the opportunity to combine patient care and clinical research. One of my main research interests was human sexuality with a special emphasis on the fertility potential of spinal injured men.

At the time of Ramon's death, the sexual function of men with spinal injuries had not been widely studied. Erections, which are a kind of reflex, could be induced with various medications as well as mechanical devices, but nothing worked reliably and patient acceptance of these aids was low. Viagra was still a long way in the future. In contrast to erections, however, ejaculation is a complex neurological event that requires coordination of several different parts of the brain. When signals from the brain are cut off by injury to the spinal cord, ejaculation can't occur. And without ejaculation, sperm can't be delivered to fertilize a woman's eggs.

"Isn't it just as well if men with spinal cord injuries can't ejaculate?" asked Dr. William Spencer, president of the hospital. We were discussing Ramon's injuries over lunch in his office a few days after the funeral service. Despite being a pioneer in rehabilitation medicine, Dr. Spencer held some old-school views.

"I mean, if the sperm are damaged, why try to retrieve them?" He cited a recent article in the medical literature about the case of a spinal-injured man in Australia.

"As I understand it," Dr. Spencer said, "doctors in Melbourne were able to obtain the man's sperm using a rectal probe. They impregnated his wife, and she delivered a badly malformed infant who died almost immediately."

I'd read the same article, which did, indeed, raise serious concerns about the health of sperm in male spinal patients. It seemed to reinforce the popular belief that the complications these patients experienced, such as infections and high fevers, inevitably damaged the sperm. Wasn't the fact that sperm are stored in the scrotum outside the body proof that this separation from bodily events protects them?

"Keep in mind, it was just one report," I said, trying to sound positive. "It could have been a coincidence. Malformed babies are born all the time."

But Dr. Spencer would have none of it. "It says to me that we shouldn't interfere with nature," he said firmly. "If these men can't have children on their own, they can always adopt."

I thought it a strange statement from a leader in the field who'd worked hard to improve the lives of the disabled. Disagreeing with my boss was always difficult, but I tried to frame the issue from a research perspective.

Rather than being the final answer, I argued, the article simply raised more questions: Were *all* sperm damaged, in *all* spinal injured men? If the sperm were damaged, what caused it and when did it happen? Most importantly, how could this problem be studied in a larger group of men?

My experience with Ramon Gutierrez helped make me aware of these questions. However, at the time of my conversation with Dr. Spencer, I wasn't prepared to study them myself—I wouldn't have known where to begin or what resources would be required.

Two years later, however, I met Dr. Stephen Seager, a veterinarian who had developed a specialty working with endangered species including pandas and great apes. To help these animals reproduce, he obtained sperm by using rectal probe electro-ejaculation. This involved inserting a customized probe into the animal's rectum and stimulating the nerves near the prostate gland with a small amount of electrical current. The technique reliably produced a large ejaculate that was then used to artificially impregnate female animals.

"It's safe, easy and effective," Dr. Seager said. "I've used it with dozens of species." When he learned that I was working with spinal cord injured men who couldn't ejaculate, he was enthusiastic. "We should try electro-ejaculation on some of your patients."

"It's a great idea," I said. "But I'm not sure the hospital will approve." I described my conversation with Dr. Spencer and the report from Australia about the malformed infant.

"We don't have to impregnate anyone," Dr. Seager replied. "All we want to show is that these men can ejaculate using this technique."

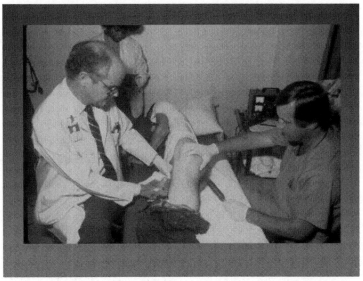

A patient undergoing rectal probe stimulation with Dr. Seager, myself, and the clinic nurse

It was a tantalizing idea, and we decided to pursue it. The first step was to get volunteers. This was easier than I'd anticipated, as every patient I asked was interested. One of these potential subjects mentioned the idea to Roberta Hatcher, a hospital social worker known around the hospital as a busybody. She got me on the phone and started a mini-inquisition. Although her concerns weren't completely unreasonable, her voice revealed a disdain for doctors and newfangled research.

"Is sticking this thing up there safe?" Hatcher asked, avoiding the word 'rectum.' "And who's this Dr. Seager guy, anyway?"

"He's a well-known veterinarian," I said. "He's been using this technique in animals for years without harm, both in the States and in Africa."

"Yeah," Hatcher said. She paused. "But it's got to be painful as hell."

"In a normal person, it would be very painful," I admitted. "But we'll only try this in spinal injured men with no sensation in the rectum."

"Who else has done this? Can't we get in trouble if we go first?"

I decided not to mention the Australian report. "As far as I know, no one else has done this before," I lied into the phone. And then I tried to reassure her. "You have to remember, this is the nature of research, trying things for the first time. How else can science advance?"

"Don't you need government approval?" This was a question naysayers often asked.

Government approval was a valid concern, I replied, though in this case, it wasn't relevant as we were not using federal funds.

Nowadays, we'd also need to have gotten approval from a local human subjects review board, but in those days, such review boards were just being developed. Researchers were allowed to proceed using their best judgment—a foolish standard but in those days accepted practice.

"I hope I've answered your questions," I said, eager to wrap up with the social worker. I'd already decided when we experimented with our first volunteer, I would make sure Hatcher wasn't at the hospital that day. "I don't want to hurt patients any more than you do," I added. "We'll go slowly, one step at a time."

The next task was selecting our first volunteer. I found him during a routine visit to the outpatient clinic.

Mike Densler was a successful, 27-year-old Houston business executive who had been injured in a motorcycle accident two years earlier and was now living with Carol Olson, his fiancée. He had a complete spinal injury at the mid thoracic level which meant he had no feeling or movement below his belly button. Since his injury, he'd taken excellent care of himself and had not experienced any infections or high fevers that could have damaged his sperm. This made him an ideal candidate, and both he and Carol were very interested in his trying the procedure when I explained it to them.

Before talking with Mr. Densler, Dr. Seager

and I had met several times to develop a preliminary research protocol. This involved a baseline physical examination, inspecting the rectum before and after the procedure to rule out any lesions, monitoring vital signs throughout the procedure and having the patient return the following day to check for any adverse effects such as pain, diarrhea or muscle spasms.

When the big day arrived, all of us in the outpatient examination room—Mike, Rhonda Bartlett, the clinic nurse, Dr. Seager and I— were excited but nervous. Mike's fiancée, Carol, had decided to wait in another room. We didn't articulate this to each other, but if this experiment was successful, it would be historic. However, history is something you only appreciate in retrospect. And if it wasn't successful? If something went wrong? We didn't discuss that either. At the time, our sole concern was patient safety. And his safety and wellbeing were my responsibility. I was the one with the proper training and credentials in human medicine; I was the captain of this impromptu team, navigating in uncharted waters without proper hospital authorization, hidden by a curtain in the outpatient clinic.

"Tell us each time you get a new reading," I said to Nurse Bartlett. She was using a manual inflatable cuff to monitor Mike's blood pressure and pulse.

"Baseline 115/75, pulse 84," she said. This was completely within normal limits. Then: "112/80 and pulse 82, holding steady."

Meanwhile, my job was to hold a small plastic cup to catch any ejaculate. *What if he screams out in pain?* I asked myself. *What if his blood pressure goes berserk? What if something happens we haven't even considered?* I thought about Travis Johnson, the high school football star who'd died of a brain hemorrhage, and about Ramon Gutierrez, the newlywed jockey, who'd taken his own life because he thought he'd never have kids. I'd failed to protect them, and here I was, deliberately doing something risky. I felt Ramon would have been pleased with our experiment, and yet my heart was racing and the little plastic cup was shaking in my hand. A failure here would be disastrous. I took a deep breath.

"Go ahead, Stephen," I said to Dr. Seager. "Turn on the juice." It was a lame attempt at humor, and no one smiled. He gently inserted a probe the size of a screwdriver handle into Mike's rectum. So far so good. Then, using a controller box, Dr. Seager slowly turned a knob to deliver a carefully calibrated number of volts.

"I'll start at 5 volts and work my way up slowly," Seager said. Then, Bartlett and Seager called out numbers.

"7 volts," he said.

"110/75, pulse 80," she answered.

"10 volts."

"115/80, pulse 76."

I leaned forward to examine Densler's eyes, looking for any wincing or other sign of pain. "How are you feeling?" I asked. He smiled.

"12 volts." We had agreed not to go higher than 25 volts—what you'd get from a few flashlight batteries.

"110/65 and 74."

This was good news...No, great news! The vital signs were stable. Even going down occasionally. I checked the plastic cup. Empty. Then up to 15 ... 16 ... and ... finally ... 18 volts. Nothing.

"Okay, I'll try 20 volts," Seager said, and at that moment Densler made a quick, involuntary movement back and forth at the hips, a kind of spasm. His penis became erect and a small amount of thick white fluid appeared at the end of his penis and fell into the plastic cup. An ejaculate!

Densler's eyes were closed, his face relaxed. He still didn't feel anything. "Look at what just happened!" I said to him. I held up the cup, which may have had one or two milliliters of sperm—just a few drops. I've never seen anyone happier.

"I can't wait to tell Carol." Two years earlier, right after his injury, he'd been told that ejaculation was one of his bodily functions that would no longer work. "Loss" became a daily curse, an unspoken four-letter word. Now, here was something vital, something at his core that had remained intact; something essential that said he was still a man.

Later that day, we examined a drop of Densler's sperm under a microscope. It was a beautiful sight. There were thousands of sperm swirling and twisting as though trying to shout "We're here!" Seager estimated the motility at 10 to 15% with a forward motion of 2 to 3+ on a scale of 0-4. While these measures were less than you might see in an uninjured man, they were nonetheless encouraging and capable of causing an impregnation. Not bad for our first effort. Although the average man may have 60, 80 or even 120 million sperm in a typical ejaculate with 50 to 60% motility, only one sperm needs to enter an egg to initiate fertilization.

After our initial success, Densler returned to the clinic three more times over the course of the next several months. Meanwhile, he and Carol had gotten married and were committed to trying to have a child. Each time we artificially ejaculated him it was easier, and his sperm count increased along with all the basic parameters of sperm health. Of course, looking at the sperm under the microscope couldn't tell us if there had been damage to his DNA. Such tests wouldn't be available for years. Nevertheless, everyone was eager to push ahead and try for a pregnancy.

*****

Despite our plans, outside events intervened. Early in the spring of 1986, just after my 50th birthday, I received an attractive offer to leave Houston and move to Washington, D.C. to be part of a team that was establishing the National Rehabilitation Hospital, a pioneering facility in the nation's capital. It was an exciting opportunity, with the added advantage of allowing my wife and me and our two daughters to live closer to our relatives and roots in the East. Over the course of the next year, I recruited Seager to join me in Washington, where we established a fertility clinic for spinal cord injured men. By a curious turn of fate, one of the first patients in the new clinic was Mike Densler. He'd recently taken a job in Northern Virginia, and he and Carol lived only 45 minutes from the hospital.

We resumed where we had left off. The quantity and quality of his sperm was as good as ever, so the next step was to have them visit a fertility clinic to have her fertility potential assessed and prepare her for artificial insemination.

In the fall of 1987 everyone was ready to proceed. We ejaculated Mike to coincide with Carol's ovulation. The sperm was carried in an insulated pocket to keep it warm while it was transported to the fertility clinic. The doctors there washed the sperm and prepared it for insemination into Carol's uterus. Everything went as smoothly as we could have hoped.

Carol called a few weeks later with the news we had waited a long time to hear: she was pregnant and doing fine. She was a healthy, 25-year-old woman and close monitoring revealed the development of a normal fetus. Nine months and one week after she was impregnated with her husband's sperm obtained with electro-ejaculation, she gave birth in a Virginia hospital. Densler called me from the delivery room. He could hardly talk but was finally able to shout, "It's a boy! A beautiful, healthy baby boy!"

For the Denslers, a beautiful baby boy; for us, proof that a simple, revolutionary method of retrieving sperm could help these men achieve their dream of having healthy biological children. The technique quickly spread to other spinal cord injury treatment centers, and led to the birth of hundreds of healthy babies in this country and around the world.

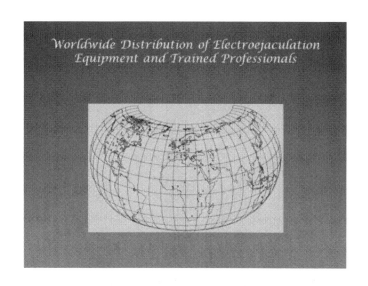

A patient with his three healthy children born through the Fertility Clinic.

Chapter Nine:
An Illness in Search of a Name

"What's the matter?" Dr. Edward Carter asked me one Wednesday morning in the fall of 1982. Carter was my boss at TIRR and each Wednesday, we walked to three nearby hospitals to evaluate patients who might be transferred to our facility. Normally, I found the two-hour walk enjoyable as well as good exercise. Today, however, something was wrong.

"I'm not feeling so hot," I lied. Actually, I felt all right except for my legs, which were strangely heavy. The idea of walking even a block seemed impossible. In truth, my legs had been feeling heavy for several weeks; more recently, the little toe on my left foot had turned numb. But I was scared. These were the classic symptoms of a slipped disc—or worse—multiple sclerosis.

Like any normal physician, my first instinct was to handle these symptoms myself. For the next month, I followed a self-prescribed program of vigorous lower-back exercises. Instead of getting better, however, the numbness in my toe gave way to a loss of feeling across half of my left foot and ankle. Finally, I decided to seek help.

The neurosurgeon I consulted, Dr. Benjamin Lockhart, couldn't see much on the X-ray, so he recommended a new imaging technique called a CAT scan. "That might give us more information," he said. "If it shows a slipped disc, we'll have to operate."

The CAT scan did show a slipped disc in my lower spine, so I was scheduled for surgery the following morning. But since CAT scans were new, the neurosurgeon ordered a repeat scan an hour before surgery to confirm the diagnosis.

"I don't get it," Dr. Lockhart said as my back was being prepped for surgery, "The second scan is clean. No disc." He paused for a moment to let this sink in. Then he added, "If you like, we can still go ahead and operate. I mean, you're prepped and ready to go. We can open you up and take a quick look around to make sure there's nothing else going on."

He sounded like an auto mechanic: Just open the hood and make a few adjustments. I declined the offer.

In the weeks that followed, nothing improved. I cut back on walking, but my legs still felt heavy. The numbness in my left foot improved but then returned. I saw one neurologist and then another, reminding each one about my history of polio. Test after test was negative. Multiple sclerosis was ruled out. Guillain-Barré was ruled out. One neurologist thought it might be amyotrophic lateral sclerosis, commonly known as Lou Gehrig's disease, but he wasn't sure. "Give it time," was all he could say.

I gave it time. I was eventually examined by some of the top doctors in Houston, but no one could explain my symptoms.

Finally, I went to one more specialist who was an international authority on amyotrophic lateral sclerosis. "We can't be a hundred percent sure," the expert said, after reviewing all my tests, "but it looks and smells like ALS." The disease is so terrifying that he wouldn't even pronounce its full name. It reminded me of a witch doctor I'd met in Nigeria who believed certain words were so powerful that to say them out loud could make someone sick.

"The numbness in your foot doesn't fit the diagnosis, but I'd say that's a red herring," he said. "There must be a pinched nerve or something in there." Maybe I should have let the neurosurgeon look under the hood after all.

"What do you recommend I do?" I could barely choke out the words. Most people with ALS died within two to three years, five at the most, and then attached to a respirator. There was no treatment, no cure, no anything; just waiting for death.

"Keep busy," the expert advised. "Go back to work. Keep your mind occupied." Nothing from his lips about the distractions of travel or advice to cherish my two young daughters or ways to find peace with my soul. Nothing. No mention of any research studies I could join or words of hope about a possible cure just around the corner. No tiny, precious shoots of false optimism sprinkled with a drop of kindness. It was American medicine at its cut-and-dried ugliest. The Nigerian witch doctor would have been a blessing by contrast.

In the days that followed, a cloud of despair enveloped me. I was 46 years old and just hitting my stride professionally. I had two beautiful daughters and a loving wife. There was a lot to live for, but suddenly it all seemed hopeless.

In the meantime, the numbness in my left foot—the red herring—went away, but the heaviness in my legs gave way to severe muscle pain in my thighs, even when I walked short distances. I started to use a motorized scooter to navigate the long hospital corridors. There was no explanation for my new symptoms and nowhere to turn.

And then it hit me: The muscle pain was not new. It felt exactly like the muscle pain I'd had when I got polio almost 30 years earlier. Was my body sending me a message from long ago? It seemed too farfetched to even contemplate. In all my extensive medical evaluations, no one had been interested in my history of poliomyelitis. Why should they be? Polio had been conquered. The polio vaccines were an unparalleled success, and research had ground to a halt. It was time to tackle more important health threats like heart disease and cancer. My own illness with polio was a distant memory—and one I preferred to forget.

The fresh insight into my muscle pain sent me to the medical library. There I found a 1972 article from the Mayo Clinic describing a group of patients with a history of polio who presented with new, unexplained weakness. The authors called it a "frustrated" form of ALS—one that wasn't as lethal since patients were living well past the allotted time of five years. Is this what I had? Why had no one mentioned this study? Had the Mayo Clinic's conclusions been proven wrong?

I decided to see if there was a follow-up study or maybe an authors' retraction. I didn't locate anything new from the Mayo Clinic on "frustrated ALS" but I did find a recent article about polio published in December 1981, by two researchers at Ohio State University. They'd done an electromyography (EMG) study which tested muscles and nerves in a group of eight or nine polio survivors. Their results were totally unexpected and suggested that as polio patients aged, their muscles and nerves started to decompensate. In other words, as individuals with a history of polio got older, this decompensation might explain new weakness. This was a pilot study and would need to be confirmed by other researchers.

Was this what was happening to me? Was

the virus coming back? Maybe not a fresh infection but a reawakening of the original virus. It wasn't common, but there were examples in medicine where something triggered a virus to become reactivated after years of lying dormant.

I had to learn more. The lead author was a young physician named David Wiechers. Before I called him, I made a list of all the questions I could think of about his study, and how it might relate to me.

"I've got the same questions, and I'm definitely not an expert in polio," he said over the telephone. "I just did an EMG study in eight people who happened to have had the disease. I was as amazed as everyone else at the findings."

Expert or not, here was someone willing to talk about my symptoms and speculate about possible causes. Our conversation lasted more than an hour, and by the end we had concluded this was a topic worth pursuing. We agreed to stay in touch.

As reassuring as my discussion with Wiechers was, I was disturbed by the fact that he hadn't observed that any of the subjects in his study were losing strength. And even more discouraging, I was the only polio survivor he had heard about who was getting weaker. So maybe my illness wasn't related to polio after all? "I can't explain it," he said. "But let's keep an open mind."

Two weeks after I hung up with Wiechers, an extraordinary thing happened. A man in his mid-50's with a history of childhood polio affecting his right leg came to see me in the outpatient clinic. I'd never seen him before.

"I don't understand, Doc," he said, "my good left leg has been getting slowly weaker over the past year." He pounded his left thigh with his fist to emphasize his frustration. "This leg has been as strong as an ox for as long as I can remember. What am I going to do?"

His story wasn't exactly the same as mine, but there were definite parallels. Was this a second case of this mysterious illness? As soon as I left the clinic, I telephoned Wiechers. He had been about to call me.

"Just this morning," he said, "I saw someone in my clinic with your exact symptoms. I'm calling it Halstead's syndrome."

We both laughed. "What a great name," I said. "But I'm not sure I want the honor. How about Halstead-Wiechers disease?"

Although our suggestions were made in jest, it raised a critical issue. Names in medicine are important. A name creates a concrete point of reference; it can tie a bow around seemingly unrelated symptoms and give them a certain dignity. A name confers credibility, which is the first step toward a wider recognition. Maybe what I was experiencing was simply an illness in search of a name.

"Anyway," Wiechers said after we joked some more about possible naming options, "it's not a laughing matter. Now there are three cases. This is no mere coincidence. There have to be more people out there. We just have to find them."

"We need to develop a plan," I agreed. I was already thinking about a research study. Find more people—dozens or even hundreds—who'd had polio.

Research was now in my blood, and fortunately, I was working in an academic setting which encouraged it. The next steps were obvious: develop a protocol, collect data, publish. This is the way science worked. In addition to patient care, this was what I had been doing for the past decade. I loved it, but the prospect of studying my own illness was scary, if thrilling. Could I be objective? What if I uncovered some unpleasant truth? Might I be biased?

I suggested several research steps and asked Wiechers what he thought.

"We need to meet," he replied. "There's too much to discuss over the phone. We need time to think this through and figure out the best way to proceed."

It was good advice.

Over the next few months, David Wiechers and I met several times. We agreed that before embarking on any formal studies, it made sense to talk to a group of "old-timers"—retired physicians who'd treated hundreds of cases of polio during the big epidemics. Perhaps some of them had witnessed polio survivors develop unexplained new weakness. Maybe it was so common that no one had thought to report it.

"It would be great to get these old guys together in a room for an afternoon," Wiechers said as we sat in my office in Houston. "Have them bounce ideas off one another. The only problem is logistics. Where would we meet? Where would everyone stay? Who would pay for it?"

"Maybe we should organize a formal meeting," I suggested. "You know, make a list of who we want to attend, write a proposal, get a grant."

Wiechers suggested that we hold it right there in Houston, and have our hospitals and the medical schools sponsor it.

As soon as he mentioned the possibility of a sponsor, it gave me another idea. "How about Warm Springs? Everyone knows about its role in treating polio," I said. "Maybe they could sponsor a meeting."

Warm Springs is the remote rehabilitation center in southern Georgia built on the site of naturally heated springs. Its name is synonymous with polio. Franklin Roosevelt convalesced there following his illness in 1921. During the big epidemics, the therapeutic waters became a Mecca for thousands of polio patients seeking to recover their health.

"Brilliant!" Wiechers said. "I've never been to Warm Springs but they say it's beautiful. It would be an ideal place to hold a meeting about polio."

During the weeks and months that followed, our ideas for the first scientific meeting about these mysterious new health problems evolved from an informal afternoon session of retired polio physicians to a structured, multidisciplinary conference of international experts that would last two and a half days. We invited leading neurologists, physiatrists, pathologists and virologists—a who's who of polio researchers and clinicians. We raised enough money from foundations and private donors to cover travel expenses as well as offer an honorarium for those who made presentations. These funds enabled us to bring in attendees from across the United States as well as from England, Canada, Europe and Australia.

At the same time that Wiechers and I were finalizing plans for the conference, we both encountered new patients with this mysterious illness. It was almost as if we'd set some unseen force in motion that brought new cases to our clinics. Clearly, this was a more common phenomenon than either of us had imagined, making the meeting all the more urgent. Instead of

"Halstead Syndrome" we now referred to it as "The Late Effects of Polio".

From the outset, our goals were modest: to convene a small medical conference in the backwater town of Warm Springs, to encourage a wide ranging discussion regarding this new phenomenon and to develop a research agenda to address basic questions such as: How many people are affected? What complaints do they have? Is this a new disease and, if so, what is the cause? The conference was meant to be a preliminary exploration of the problem and the last thing we wanted was premature publicity. Science is a jealous mistress and treasures her privacy.

However, it was not to be. Just before lunch on the last day of the conference, I got word that someone wanted to speak with me in an outside room. Expecting to meet with one of the Warm Springs' administrators or perhaps a participant who had to leave early, I was confronted instead by a room full of reporters. Someone had tipped off the press that there was a 'secret' conference on polio. Rumors had spread and now there was fear that polio was back.

Are we going to see new epidemics? Is it safe to send my kid to school? Do we need to find another vaccine? The questions were endless. While there were no definitive conclusions from the conference, most participants believed the new symptoms were related to aging. A few hypothesized there was a reactivation of the virus. No one was predicting new epidemics—this was a health problem confined exclusively to people who'd had the disease earlier in life.

I tried to emphasize these points with the reporters. Still, it was big news. Most Americans hadn't forgotten the terrifying epidemics of the mid-20th century. The specter of polio still had the power to fascinate and create fear. The day following the conference, there were front-page stories in all the major newspapers. While there was some reckless speculation, most of the news articles gave an honest, balanced account of the scientific presentations. The headline in the *The New York Times* was typical and read: "Some Polio Symptoms May Recur up to 40 Years after the Disease." There was no mention of a virus on the loose or need to keep the kids home from school. The message in the *Times* was simple: this was a new problem for some polio patients and it required more research.

*****

The conference was held in May 1984 and had exceeded our wildest expectations—it had a historic, worldwide impact that changed forever our understanding of the polio experience.

The burst of publicity had another unexpected consequence. As the news spread to every corner of the country, tens of thousands of polio survivors, who for decades hadn't wanted anything to do with another person with polio, began networking to organize support groups in their communities. People met to share stories and coping strategies, as well as to invite physicians to give updates on the newest research. By 1990, barely six years after the Warm Springs Conference, there were over 300 post-polio support groups in this country and many more in developed countries around the world.

With so many patients asking questions, the research community responded with enthusiasm and money. During the thirty years following the Warm Springs conference, hundreds of research projects were funded in this country and abroad and the results published widely. The illness that had been in search of a name became known around the world as post-polio syndrome.

*****

All of the scientific and lay activity inspired by the conference was a high water mark in my career as a physician. In the early 1990's, the federal government estimated that there were two million people in this country with a history of polio. As many as a quarter of them were believed to be experiencing post-polio syndrome—more than either those with multiple sclerosis or ALS. Since then, with the passage of time, the post-polio population has steadily declined as age and other illnesses have taken their toll.

Although no effective drugs for post-polio syndrome have been discovered, polio researchers and clinicians have been able to develop strategies to manage the weakness, pain and fatigue many patients experience. In addition to my contributions to the medical literature, I take enormous pride in having been able to offer to patients in my clinic many of the insights I gained from my own experience with this illness. This has provided me the privilege of being able to treat my patients with an extra measure of credibility and empathy.

Friendships with Men

Chapter Ten:
Cold Beer in Houston

The 1960's and 1970's in this country were a period of social ferment. In addition to protesting the war in Vietnam, many of those who'd been previously marginalized by society were energized to assert their rights. The widespread availability of birth control in the early 1960's had freed women sexually, which led to demands that they be in control of all aspects of their lives from the bedroom to the boardroom. The iconic women's health manual, *Our Bodies, Ourselves*, became both a "how-to" book and a Bible. In cities across the country, "Take Back the Night" marches raised awareness of issues regarding women's self-determination and led to the development of specific plans of action in the workplace and the home. Consciousness raising, or CR, groups enabled women to share their ideas and experiences and support one another in their efforts to take their rightful place in a liberated society. My wife, Kris, joined one such CR group soon after we moved to Houston in 1973. It was such a positive and powerful experience for her that I was inspired to help start a CR group for men.

One evening I got together with Frank, the husband of one of the women in my wife's CR group, and another friend, Andy, to discuss forming our own CR group. Frank and I had been envious of the beneficial effects of the consciousness raising experience on our wives, but now, as we sipped cold beer in Frank's living room, Andy wondered aloud what we would talk about.

"I don't know," Frank said. "We can talk about anything you want." Silence filled the room as we stared at our bottles, struggling for something meaningful to say. Fortunately, the room was dark so we couldn't see each other's embarrassed expressions.

"I don't know how the British do it," I said at last.

"Do what?"

"Drink warm beer," I replied.

"Well," Frank said after a long pause. "You know, we don't have to talk about anything special."

Another awkward silence. "Okay. Who wants another cold one?"

There was brief, nervous laughter. Here we were, three adult men trying to start a group to share feelings, and all we could talk about was beer. We sat in the dark for a long time, our faces hidden, clutching empty beer bottles, desperate to say something. Anything. Anything at all.

I cleared my throat. "Maybe we need more members," I said. "With a larger group, we'll have more ideas."

The other two suddenly came to life. "Great suggestion," Andy said. "How about if each of us invites two others?"

Men like action and here was an action plan. We had another beer and then gave each other a firm handshake. Our action plan didn't include hugs.

Many of those we invited attended a session or two and then dropped out, citing a lack of time or inability to make a weekly commitment. But I think the real reason they'd dropped out was fear: fear of the unknown, fear of talking openly with other men about personal issues, and fear that such a group might uncover an uncomfortable attraction to other men. Although psychologists have long noted that human beings experience both homosexual and heterosexual attraction, men have been particularly disturbed by this idea. In what was, in those days, a strongly homophobic society, even emotional closeness between two men was considered abnormal. This was especially true in the Bible belt, where being macho was a prized virtue.

Eventually, though, we found ten men who seemed compatible and were willing to meet every Thursday evening for several hours to share experiences and feelings. It was not a therapy group and there was no formal leader. Instead, we took turns setting the weekly agenda and leading the meeting. This way, we each had an opportunity to bring up the topics we wanted to discuss.

Frank and I were physicians and Andy a medical student, though our group also included a Greek immigrant who managed a flower shop, a kindergarten teacher, a graduate student in sociology, an office worker in the Merchant Marines, an auto mechanic and two oil company executives. Our ages ranged from early 50's to late 20's (I was 42); five of us were married, two divorced, and the others single. No one admitted to being a homosexual although two said they had had sex with another man.

The group met weekly for more than two years, with increasing momentum and commitment. This exciting intellectual and emotional journey became so compelling to most of us that calendars were rearranged and travel plans cancelled. Perhaps the best thing about our meetings was the easy camaraderie we felt in each other's presence. There was no pressure to perform or to be the smartest guy in the room. Personal growth was the mutual goal, with everyone progressing at his own speed. It was understood that our discussions were confidential and as the weeks rolled by we became increasingly comfortable sharing intimate details of our lives. Most of us had never been in such a group before, much less had an opportunity to share our inner lives, week after week, with other men. The stars had aligned and for a while we were a band of brothers, sharing the experience of a lifetime.

Discussion topics included women, dating, parents, careers and our own childhoods. We talked about our relationships with siblings and who, in our families, was the favored child. Nothing was taboo except politics and religion. The idea was to stay focused on what it was like to grow up and be a man in our particular moment in American history. This didn't mean, however, that we were serious all the time. Once we had a costume party where each of us dressed as a person from history or literature. Because I'd lived in Italy for a year and loved foreign travel, I wore robes to look like Marco Polo. Others came dressed as Robin Hood, King Henry VIII and Benjamin Franklin. Other activities included a reading of someone's favorite play, or gathering in the kitchen of a member who loved to cook while he prepared his favorite dishes for us.

One evening we went to a sports bar where we played pool, ping-pong and shot hoops on a nearby basketball court. Since pool and basketball both require two hands, I stood on the sidelines and watched the others play. But I'd learned to play one-handed ping-pong in college after my illness, so I had the satisfaction of beating everyone in our group in a tournament. Disability had helped me learn to pick battles where I could do well.

Later, after the sports bar, we retired to Andy's apartment where we talked about how competition can dominate men's lives, for better or worse. As if on cue, one of the guys revealed that he had kept a secret tally of winners and losers. This led to a discussion of which game was the most important and the basic unfairness of scorekeeping, especially in the game of life.

Toward the end of that evening, the young kindergarten teacher, who had been rather quiet, said, "Tonight was very tough for me." He was sitting off by himself in a corner of the room. "It brought back memories of when I was in school. I wasn't very athletic and the older kids used to bully me." His voice dropped to a whisper and then he began to cry. Several men went over to sit next to him. "And then..." He put his head in his hands and fell to the floor in a fetal position. After a long silence, he said simply, "Vietnam... I couldn't take it... They bullied me... I tried to commit suicide."

We sat there, stunned. None of us knew what to say. Then, one by one, we went over to where he was on the floor and took turns lying next to him, giving him wordless hugs.

Not every meeting ended with hugs. We were just ten guys, after all, with strong personalities and a full capacity for petty squabbles and flashes of temper. All of us were coping with different challenges on our journey through life, journeys that often left us exhausted at the end of a long day. Occasionally, someone would show up and drink a beer or two, stretch out on the floor with his eyes closed and take a brief nap.

My own journey had taken a decidedly positive turn in recent years. I was several years into my second marriage, which had produced two young daughters. At the same time, the women's movement had influenced my wife to change her career and to question the traditional gender roles in our marriage. Although this created a good deal of tension in our marriage, in the long run it ultimately resulted in a strengthening of our relationship. I was happy with my career at the rehabilitation hospital and felt fulfilled in a job that suited my temperament and training. Because I was experiencing a good deal of personal satisfaction, however, I unfortunately misjudged how difficult life was for others in the group.

On the night we met at my house, it was my turn to establish the agenda. By then, we'd explored a number of challenging topics including lying, stealing and sex. I thought that since we'd talked about sex, we could talk about anything.

"My topics for this evening are work, work satisfaction and income," I said to the group.

We were sitting on large, comfortable cushions in a circle on the floor in the sunroom at the back of my house. I started the discussion by describing my journey to find myself as a physician. Although I'd had moments of despair and doubt, it was basically a feel-good story. Regardless of how much I may have struggled, becoming a physician in this society is still a mark of high accomplishment. Who wouldn't want to be a doctor?

Because fortune had smiled on me, I blithely assumed it had smiled on the rest of the group as well. In my hubris, I forgot how well we hide our own struggles and how much a man's identity and sense of self-worth is often equated with the status of his job and his financial success.

"Who wants to go next and say something about their job?" I asked.

The others sat in silence for a few moments, avoiding each other's anxious glances.

"It's no secret. I hate my job and I hate my life," blurted out Phillip, who had a desk job with the Merchant Marines. He looked at the faces of the men sitting around him. "As far as I can tell, the rest of you guys have got it made. Me, I'm going nowhere. My dream had been to go to sea but I flunked my physical and now I'm stuck in an office for the rest of my life."

"If you hate your job, you should try mine for a while," Kenny, the auto mechanic, said.

"Christ, all I do all day are menial lube jobs for business executives and frustrated housewives. I'm certified to do foreign cars, which I really like, but they all go to the boss's son."

Those of us who liked our jobs tried to understand their frustration and anger, but it was difficult and painfully awkward. These guys were trapped in dead-end, unfulfilling jobs. Though we all agreed that life is unfair, and none of us had walked in their shoes, we couldn't help wondering whether they had taken full advantage of all their opportunities.

Instead of taking the hint that this conversation was going nowhere, I continued with my oblivious, tone-deaf leadership role.

"I know," I said to the group. "Instead of talking about our jobs and careers, why don't we just share what we make? I'll start and we can go around the circle."

It was a foolish, ignorant, selfish, and egotistical proposal. Why would anyone want to talk about his salary if he hated his job and was feeling trapped? Nevertheless, I blundered on, giving an approximation of my income. I turned to Frank, who was sitting next to me. He was a self-employed pediatrician who stated a figure that was considerably higher than I would have guessed. I began to wonder if people would tell the truth, when I should have focused on the emotional stress I was causing. We got halfway around the circle to Phillip. He stared at us in silence and then started to stutter.

"Well ... I ... I," he said. Then, without uttering another sound, he jumped to his feet and disappeared out the sliding glass door of the sunroom. Just beyond the door was a backyard pool and suddenly there was a loud splash.

"What the hell's he doing?" Kenny said and went over to the open door. He gave a loud shout of astonishment as he saw Phillip splashing around fully clothed in our backyard pool.

"What kind of a fool is he?" Frank asked.

"Don't worry," I said. "It's a small pool. He's just trying to cool off." Obviously, it was much more than that. Jumping into the water that night was the result of years of frustration and anger which had been building for Phillip's entire life.

It was the last time any of us saw Phillip. To our shame, we were too upset and embarrassed to discuss what had happened, so we just said our goodbyes and everyone went home. The following week was no better. We probably all felt some guilt, but I felt guiltiest of all. This was a clear example of how a trained leader could have provided some useful guidance. To my regret, I never took responsibility for what had happened that evening, but I did learn that a man's income should be added to politics and religion on the list of taboo subjects. No one ever mentioned Phillip's name again. It had also become taboo. It was as if we'd been on a ship together and, in the night, without a sound, a wave had washed him overboard. It was the low point in our journey together. But there were other times when we stood tall and helped facilitate important life changes.

Among our different personalities, Ronald, the graduate student, was the shyest. He didn't have a girlfriend and often complained about how lonely he was.

"I've got an idea how to help you," I said one night. "However, you've got to promise to do exactly as I say." Everyone looked at me, puzzled. "Here's the deal," I continued, "and everybody here's a witness." I pulled out a prescription pad and scribbled some words. I then handed the prescription to Ronald who read it out loud.

"Diagnosis: congenitally shy; unable to meet girls. Treatment: strike up a conversation with a different girl each day for five days. Report back to us in one week."

We all laughed, but I hoped my prescription would turn out to be exactly what Ronald needed. To cure his shyness, he had to follow doctor's orders, and if he didn't like the treatment, he could blame it on the group. At the next meeting the following week, Ronald was the first to arrive.

"You'll never believe what happened," he

said with a big smile. "I approached five different girls and I got the names of two of them." He held up a piece of paper. "Here's their names and phone numbers." We gave him a round of applause and then, one by one, gave him a hug. That night he was the happiest man in Houston. He had found his courage. A year later, Ronald was going steady with a woman who lived in his apartment complex. It was an illustration of the power of the group to influence, inspire and support change in its members.

But the best example of this transformative power happened to the oldest member, Patrick, one of the oil executives. Pat had been initially hesitant to join our group, fearing it would be too "touchy-feely." He was married with three children and comfortably settled in upper-class Houston society. At the initial meetings, while the rest of us were dressed casually in T-shirts and jeans and sat on the floor, Pat wore a jacket and tie and sat stiffly in a chair. He was physically there, but emotionally absent.

And yet, our meetings must have had some meaning for him, as he returned week after week. Eventually, we were able to convince him to loosen his tie and remove his jacket. Then one evening, he showed up in a pair of new blue jeans and sat among us on the floor. We all toasted his progress while he flashed a sheepish grin. Not long afterwards, we learned additional details about his children. Two were married and had successful careers while the youngest, Ben, was, in his words, "an irresponsible hippie."

"For a while, he was living on a beach in Hawaii with some woman he picked up," Pat told us one evening with barely concealed contempt. "He was nothing but a bum selling driftwood and surviving on handouts."

But as time passed, we learned that this was not the full story. We later found out that Ben had managed to buy a small fishing boat and had moved to Alaska, where he was a commercial fisherman. He'd married the woman from Hawaii and they had a small son, Pat's first grandchild. The 'bum' story was far more complex than Pat had led us to believe.

"When's the last time you were in touch with Ben?" the shy graduate student, Ronald, asked. He might have been about the same age as Ben.

"It's been a long time," Pat said. "Maybe seven, maybe eight years."

"Jesus Christ," Frank, the pediatrician, exclaimed. "Seven years is a long time. He's obviously changed a lot. I'll bet you wouldn't even recognize him."

"It sounds to me," Ronald said, "that your anger won't let you see the man he has become.

Wouldn't you like at least to hold and kiss your grandson?"

That did it. Pat, the successful executive, hid his face in his hands and started to sob. None of us said a word. We simply sat there and watched the years of anger, disappointment and sadness pour out into the room. Pat cried steadily for about five minutes, then took out a handkerchief and wiped his eyes.

"Thank you," he said quietly. "Thank you. That's been a long time coming. And I couldn't have done it without you guys." A long pause. "I couldn't … I couldn't have done it … without … your love." He started to sob again, his shoulders shaking. There wasn't a dry eye in the room. "Love" was not a word oil executives tossed around lightly.

Later, the group suggested he reach out to Ben by writing a letter. The idea was to keep it simple, to ask how he and his wife and child were doing. To say that he missed him, and, above all, that he loved him.

Pat wrote a letter to his son the next day and then brought it to the group to read. "I miss you, Ben, my long-lost son," the letter ended. "I hope I can see you and your family soon. Love, Dad."

Although the circumstances were very different, it reminded me of my own father and our emotional reconnection a few years earlier in Vermont that I describe in another chapter.

And now there was added satisfaction of knowing that I had helped another father and son rediscover one another before it was too late, while they were both still alive.

It was the beginning of dramatic changes in Pat's life. His son wrote back a letter that revealed a young man who was thoughtful and fully engaged in running a successful fishing business off the coast of Alaska. Gone was the rebellious hippie and, in his place, was a loving son eager for reconciliation.

Pat and his son exchanged letters and phone calls and eventually he flew to Alaska for a visit. The group was delighted but could hardly have anticipated what was to happen next. One Thursday evening Patrick arrived at the group with an important announcement.

"This is my last meeting," he said, with evident pleasure. "After 23 years, I've given my notice at the company and my wife and I are leaving Houston." We were dumbfounded. This was the same guy who'd been reluctant to loosen his tie.

"We're moving to Alaska to be near my son and his family. We're going to get a parcel of land through the Homestead Act and I'm going to build a log cabin." He let this sink in and then said, "That's right. We're going to simplify our lives and live in a log cabin. Maybe even learn to live off the land." There was no end of tears and hugs that evening.

We met a few more times after that, but the group seemed to have lost its energy. It had lasted a little over two years and had been successful beyond measure. To honor Phillip, and all the members who had come and gone, we held one more celebratory meeting, one sunny afternoon in my backyard pool. In between jumping into the refreshing water, everyone had a chance to enjoy plenty of cold beer.

Chapter Eleven:
Goodbye, Dear Friend, My Hugh

American culture has not made it easy for men to develop close relationships with other men. Little boys are given medals for being strong and swift. There are no prizes for showing your feelings and those who do are labeled "crybabies" or "wimps." As boys grow into men, they become ever more skilled at concealing their emotions, and many fail to cultivate the inner life that would enrich the person they want to become. Everything, it seems, conspires to reinforce this behavior: competition in sports, at school and at work, make it harder for men to nurture others as well as themselves. But close, intimate friendships between men, while rare, are not impossible. And when such a friendship does develop, it is like a special gift from the gods. During my life, I have been fortunate to have had many good male friends. But I have had only one friend who was handed to me by the gods. His name was Hugh Gallagher.

*****

"Wait till you see him," swooned Patricia. "He's simply divine."

"He's like a movie star," said Joy. "The most handsome man I've ever met. And smart as can be."

"He'll be here tomorrow afternoon," Patricia exclaimed excitedly.

Patricia and Joy, both in their mid-twenties, were the sisters of my college friend, Lorenzo, who came from a wealthy Florida family. The girls seemed to be anticipating the arrival of a handsome young prince at their family's beach house just south of Jacksonville. I'd been invited to spend several weeks there during the summer of 1955.

Lorenzo had contracted polio in 1953, a year before I did, while he was at Yale. For part of his recovery, he was a patient at the rehabilitation hospital in Warm Springs, Georgia, where he'd met Hugh. They'd bonded over English history, the *New York Times* crossword puzzle, and the fact that they were both struggling to recover from a serious bout of polio.

Patricia and Joy had met Hugh during a visit to Warm Springs and had been smitten.

The following afternoon, a red convertible pulled into the driveway. The top was down and behind the wheel, in the bright, Florida sunshine, sat Hugh. Tanned and full of enthusiasm, it was all there on that sunny afternoon: intelligence, wit, charm, and clever repartee. I could see how the girls might think he was divine.

The sisters descended on the convertible and exchanged hugs and kisses while he remained behind the steering wheel. As a result of his bout with polio, Hugh lost the use of his legs and his arms were weak. He could get out of the car, but it required an enormous effort. There was a heavy manual wheelchair wedged behind the driver's seat which required all his strength to lift and position it onto the driveway so that he could slide into it from the car. Although someone could have easily taken the wheelchair out of the convertible for him, polio survivors preferred to do that kind of thing by themselves to prove their independence.

After the excitement of his arrival had subsided, Joy brought out some snacks and iced tea to the car. We all sat around in lawn chairs while Hugh chatted and kidded with the girls about boyfriends and dating and the joys of hanging out on the beach. Then he had to leave. He was driving to Warm Springs for an annual checkup. He and I had barely exchanged two words.

Although I agreed with the sisters' assessment that he was handsome and very intelligent, I was distracted by thoughts of a young woman I'd met recently who was planning to fly down to Florida to join me for the weekend. There was nothing in that fleeting afternoon encounter with Hugh to suggest what was in our future: that he would become a best friend, a trusted confidante, and that together we would author an enduring bond that would span five decades.

During those five decades, our lives intersected twice in Washington, DC. The first time was while I completed my postgraduate training in internal medicine between 1964 and 1967; the second happened twenty years later when I moved to Washington permanently in 1986.

When I got in touch with Hugh, in 1964, I discovered he was beginning to fulfill the bright future many had predicted for him. He'd completed college in California and won a prestigious scholarship to study for two years at Oxford University. When he came back to the States, he worked on Capitol Hill as a legislative aide to a Senator from Colorado and had begun writing *Advise and Obstruct,* a book about the Senate which was later shortlisted for a Pulitzer Prize.

Our friendship during those three years was in a formative stage—close but not intimate. What we realized only later was that for a friendship to grow, two friends must learn to part the waters of time and hold back the tide of other commitments.

In the meantime, my life was ruled by a grueling on-call schedule at several local hospitals, while Hugh was caught up in his government day job and the swirl of evening activities expected of one of the city's eligible bachelors. Still, we did manage to meet occasionally for dinner, and little by little, the fabric of our friendship grew stronger.

Over these dinners, we talked about politics, history and love. Especially love. My dating life was focused on finding a marriage partner. He, on the other hand, was dating to keep up appearances. Behind the eligible-bachelor illusion, he struggled to come to terms with the hard reality of being homosexual in 1960's DC. His secret life created enormous tension, and in due course led to steady, mostly solitary drinking.

Although I couldn't articulate it at the time, I was dealing with my own tension regarding love and romance. During college, I'd met a special girl and formed a relationship I thought would last a lifetime. Although I was in love, I was unable to tell her that in so many words, a failing I had learned from my father. It cost me dearly.

*****

After five passionate and—I'd thought—monogamous years, I finally got up the courage in 1960, during my first year in medical school, to write to her declaring my love and asking her to marry me. It was not meant to be.

On the very day—perhaps the very hour—she received my letter, I received one from her, announcing her love for another and her plans to marry him in a few months. Like Hugh, she'd been leading a double life. Five full years of devotion were gone in the blink of an eye. Can passion die so quickly? I nursed that wound for far too long.

Five years later, in 1965, while I was doing my

postgraduate medical residency in Washington, I dated whenever I could take time off from my duties at the hospital. But I wasn't looking for love; I wanted a spouse. Love was scary and I'd been spooked. I didn't understand any of this at the time, of course, and Hugh, my sole confidante, was lost in his own world of pretty, young men and one-night stands.

But I got what I wanted: my own pretty, young woman.

Her name was Joscelind.

We married in 1966, not long after my 30th birthday, in a frantic dash to catch the crest of our infatuation that masqueraded as love. It was a disaster from the beginning—maybe even while our vows still hung in the air. She was a fine woman, but she didn't want me; she wanted a rich doctor, and I had no interest in becoming a wealthy physician in the suburbs.

The truth is that I didn't really want her, either—I wanted my college girlfriend. I wanted someone I could love. If I only knew how. We had our first argument as we climbed into the back seat of the limousine en route to our reception. It was a short ride from there to a divorce court four years later.

My path crossed with Hugh's again twenty years later in 1986. We'd both experienced adversity and challenges since the mid-1960's, but they were in the past and now our lives were in full flower. Hugh had quit the U.S. government and was working as a lobbyist for British Petroleum while writing books on the side. Before leaving his job at the Senate, he'd authored—behind the scenes—the law requiring all government buildings in the United States to be accessible to persons with disabilities. It was one of his proudest accomplishments. Another accomplishment—perhaps even more difficult—was making peace with his sexuality. He'd moved to the suburbs, where he was living and dating on his own terms as a slightly gray and openly gay man.

For my part, I was leaving Houston after thirteen years to help establish the National Rehabilitation Hospital, the first facility of its kind in the nation's capital. The years in Houston had been happy ones, and had given me unparalleled opportunities for personal and professional growth. My two daughters, Larissa and Christina, had been born there and my second wife, Kris, had found an abundance of personal and professional satisfaction. Now, however, we were traveling in different directions. Soon after moving to Washington, Kris and I decided, after seventeen years of marriage, on an amicable separation.

With so much upheaval in my life, my old friend Hugh was an anchor. We met for dinner occasionally, but quickly discovered that each of us wanted more. We were hungry for each other's company. So we started to meet once a month. Soon, it was every other week and finally we began to have dinner every Tuesday evening.

Our friendship shifted to a different plane: A compulsion. A necessity. A love.

Our time together became an oasis amidst the turmoil of daily life. Governments fell, lovers were discarded, birthdays were celebrated. The world turned on its axis and we had our weekly dinners—stepping stones toward grace.

What did we talk about?

There was the booming gay life in Washington and AIDS. There was my divorce and remarriage to my third and current wife, Jessica. There was the stale bread and slow table service where we were having supper. There was his sister in Africa and his ill father in Bethesda. Then there were urgent things to say about current events and the kings of England. Religion, race, the nature of evil, the cause of World War I. He was a scholar of European history; I was a lover of English literature. As a teenager, he'd lived in Greece. After college, I'd lived in Italy. He had been in an iron lung for months; I had been in one for several weeks. He had been on safari in Africa. I had worked with the World Health Organization in Nigeria. He'd traveled frequently to Alaska and written a book about Alaskan statehood. I'd traveled to Japan and climbed Mount Fuji. It was fascinating with what seemed like endless parallel adventures.

My bride, Jessica Scheer, on our wedding day.
February 22, 1992.

We talked about our experiences with polio
and our loss of strength; my disability and his
struggle to remain independent. There was his
book about the Third Reich and, a few years
later, his pioneering book about the impact of
polio on FDR's life and politics. There was my
third child, my son, Alexander. We had so much
to share it was hard to contain it all in the
cramped space between hello and goodbye.

Every week there was a full plate of erudition,
witticisms, obscure quotes, outrageous ideas,
unresolved arguments, one-upsmanship—an
embracing of each other's life force. I would

leave the table exhausted yet exhilarated. And always, when we parted, I felt emotionally refreshed, intellectually renewed.

Unlike other relationships I'd had with men, however, this was not about competition. It was about affection, caring and love: not eros but agape, the Greek concept of brotherly, godly love. It was a feast for the soul that sometimes didn't need words. Not everyone in life gets to have such a friend. I was lucky. I had Hugh.

And then came death and dying.

He drank heavily—mostly red wine—and more than I realized. I never saw him drunk as he drank mostly alone and quietly, late at night. He developed cirrhosis of the liver and then cancer of the colon. The cancer spread to his liver and his doctors confused it with his cirrhosis. Since getting polio at age nineteen, he'd distrusted doctors and didn't like them meddling in his life. It was an unfortunate aversion that deprived him of proper medical care when he needed it most.

Before his cancer and even before his cirrhosis, we'd talked at length about dying. He'd said he didn't want any heroic measures taken, and was emphatic about wanting to die in his own bed in his own home. As his friend, and not as a doctor, I had promised to help him in any way I could to achieve that goal.

Unfortunately, it was a promise I couldn't keep. When he became quite sick, word spread quickly among his vast army of friends, and everyone wanted to be at his bedside.

On the day before he died, I left work early and hurried to his home. When I opened the door of his living room where he lay in a hospital bed, I was greeted with a blast of voices from a throng of twenty or thirty people all talking at once. Where was the peace and tranquility this holy man deserved? When I was finally able to push my way to his bedside, his spirit was barely visible. He was *in extremis* with only hours left on this sorrowful planet. I held his hand and wept. What else could I do for my dear friend, my Hugh?

Everyone in the room that day was his friend. Everyone wished him well. Everyone wanted to do something—anything—to help. So someone picked up the phone and called an ambulance.

"He needs to be in the hospital," a friend said.

"He's dying," I said with reluctance. It was difficult to form the words. How do you say such a thing about a loved one?

I took a deep breath. "Please, everyone," I was frantic. A few people looked at me with suspicion. "Please, listen to me. Hugh's last wish is to be here ... to die in his own bed ... at home."

"How do you know what he wants?" someone asked.

"We can't just let him die here," another said.

"He belongs in a hospital where they can save him," a third voice urged.

Maybe among all those friends gathered there that day, I knew best what his final wishes were. But my voice was drowned in a sea of false hope. The army of friends had become a mob, a mob that wanted action and wouldn't listen to reasoned judgement.

In no time, the ambulance arrived. Events spun out of control. He was placed on a stretcher and hustled out the door. Barely breathing.

The next time I saw him was like a crucifixion. In the last few years of his life, he'd become a vocal advocate for dying with dignity—especially on behalf of the disabled and the disenfranchised. Now, here he was, this brave, disabled soul, in intensive care, hooked up to half a dozen tubes. Doctors and nurses, fully gowned and masked, crowded about his bed. There was no dignity in his dying and, certainly, none in his death. I turned on my heel and hurried from the hospital.

Goodbye, dear Hugh. Goodbye, dear friend.

Hugh Gregory Gallagher, 1932-2004

A Love of Music

Chapter Twelve:
Music for Life

"What are you going to play, Tommy?" a classmate called out to me from the back of the high
school auditorium at Phillips Academy. Musician friends sometimes called me 'Tommy," referring to Tommy Dorsey, the trombone-play-
ing bandleader of the 1930's and 40's known
for his smooth, mellow sound. Phillips Academy or Andover is a venerable, four-year college preparatory school located in Andover,
Massachusetts which I attended for my last two
years of high school. I had been playing the
trombone since seventh grade and in May
1953—one month before graduation—I participated in the annual school music competition,
which required one solo on a musical instrument.

The first prize was $25.

In late May, several dozen students and I
gathered in the auditorium on the Andover
campus to play our solos before a handful of
faculty and parents.

"Hey, Tommy," my classmate shouted at me
again. "What's it going to be, *Blue Skies*?" He
was referring to the famous Dorsey recording
made with Frank Sinatra. There was a ripple of
laughter.

"No, not Dorsey," I called back. "Something

from a guy named Honegger."

"Honegger?" my friend said. "Who's that?"

"He's a Swiss composer you've never heard of. And I'm going to play one of his songs you've never heard of." Picking Arthur Honegger—whom I'd known nothing about—hadn't been my idea but that of my teacher, William 'Bill' Schneider, the Andover music instructor. He'd chosen a piece from one of Honegger's oratorios a few months earlier.

"It's a little modern and definitely not well known in this country," he'd explained. "But it's the kind of piece that, if you can play it well, will stand out in a competition." He handed me a copy of the sheet music. "Give it a try. It's not easy to play, so the judges will give you extra points for degree of difficulty."

For the next two months, Bill and I met each Wednesday afternoon to practice the Honegger piece, while he played piano accompaniment. He was right about how hard it was to play— especially for a student with my academic pressures who wasn't able to practice every day. The piece started on an impossibly high note and then jumped around, high, low, sometimes *forte* and sometimes *pianissimo*. There was no discernible melody, which certainly wouldn't make it a crowd-pleaser. I didn't particularly care for it as a piece of music, nor did I like the way I kept playing so many wrong notes.

When the competition was only three weeks

away, I told Bill—not for the first time—that I didn't think I should be playing this piece. It was over my head.

"Nonsense," he replied. "You're making better progress than you realize. You'll do fine." His words didn't reassure me. I became even more nervous as Bill struggled to explain what I needed to do to improve. He was a pianist and didn't really understand how to teach a brass instrument. So his reassurances sounded hollow and made me long for my first trombone teacher, Victor DiSalvo, a tough but brilliant teacher who'd have known exactly how to guide me through the difficult passages of Honegger while giving them a winning flair.

"How much do you practice?" Mr.DiSalvo had asked me, the first time we met. I was 11 years old and in the seventh grade; my mother had brought me to his home where he taught his private students. We sat on a couch covered by a clear plastic sheet which protected the colorful floral design from any contact with the outside world. Mrs. Sofia DiSalvo, who didn't appear to speak much English, remained standing while she served everyone iced tea.

"What do you mean?" I said finally, in answer to his question, though I knew perfectly well what he meant.

"I mean," he replied firmly, "how much do you practice *every day*?" Mr. DiSalvo was short and had a black mustache which made him look a little like a young Arturo Toscanini, the famous Italian conductor.

"Every day?" I repeated, stalling for time. I took a sip of iced tea.

"Yes. Every day." He was losing patience. "For example, how much did you practice yesterday?"

I looked at my scuffed shoes. "Well... uhm..." The truth was, of course, that I hadn't practiced yesterday; nor the day before that. I didn't practice at all. No one had ever expected me to practice, so I didn't.

"Do you want to take lessons with me?" The mustache twitched.

I looked at my shoes again. "Well... Yes sir...I guess," I mumbled. "That's why my mother brought me here."

"If you want to take lessons with me," Mr. DiSalvo said, "it's real simple. There's only one rule."

"Yes sir," I looked up from my shoes. "What's that?"

"Practice," he said kindly but firmly. "If you want to take lessons from me, you have to practice. Every day. If you don't practice, find someone else. It's that simple."

It was always Mr. DiSalvo, never Victor; and always Mrs. DiSalvo, never Sofia. He was a gifted professional trombone player, who'd played with the likes of Harry James, Benny Goodman, and even Tommy Dorsey, who was his god. As good as he was, Mr. DiSalvo never reached the top, so he'd given up his grueling career of one-night stands in dance halls and orchestra pits to raise a family and teach in public schools.

After I'd been taking lessons with him for a couple of years, Mr. DiSalvo started calling me 'Tommy'—partly in jest but also as a compliment. Although he was generous in praising my playing, he never went so far as to urge me to apply to a music school like Juilliard or Eastman. He was aware of my limitations as a musician as well as the arduous climb for even a very talented musician to make it to the top. But his insistence on self-discipline turned me from a common workhorse into a proud thoroughbred that had a lasting influence on my life and the way I approached challenges.

Mr. DiSalvo was not mean, but he did believe in discipline; he'd learned its value in the Army during the war. Although I didn't appreciate it at the time, he was as much a teacher of life lessons as of music: doing well demands preparation and self-discipline; superior performance requires focusing mind and body; and hard work is its own enjoyment. Maybe that's the essence of all great teachers: by tutoring you in their craft you learn about yourself and how to reach beyond your grasp.

He started me off practicing fifteen minutes a day. To ensure that I met this modest goal, he had my mother sign a weekly practice sheet. I began with the basics: holding one note at a time as long as I could and then playing simple, five-note scales. Fifteen minutes became half an hour and then 45 minutes, and eventually I wasn't practicing but playing for enjoyment for several hours at a time. The more I played, the better I became. And the better I became, the more I enjoyed practicing. It was an upward spiral. Also, I learned the healing power of music. Whenever I was feeling discouraged or sick, I found that playing my favorite tunes for an hour or so was better than any medicine. Neurological research has confirmed my long-ago observations: in addition to helping regulate heart and respiratory rates, playing music releases endorphins and can enhance executive functions as well as brain plasticity, which modifies neural pathways and synapses.

By the time I got to Andover for my final two years of high school, I was good enough to join the two elite musical ensembles at the school: the dance band and the brass choir. However, regular practicing had to give way to required sports and academics. By now it was clear that I was not headed for a professional career in music, and I needed to be thinking of another vocation. Studying trumped practicing music, and my playing deteriorated.

It was against this background that I prepared for the school's annual music competition. I was to be one of nine soloists that afternoon: two trumpeters, two clarinetists, two pianists, and one each on the flute and violin as well as myself on the trombone. Before anyone had played a note, Bill Schneider had confided to me his opinion of each of the soloists.

"Most of the competition is pretty weak today," he said. "They're young rich kids who don't practice. They're playing to please their wealthy parents." I looked around at the crowd behind me to see if I could see who he meant. Among the twenty-five or thirty people in attendance, I recognized only a few students and one or two faculty members.

"There are only three who will give you a run for your money," Mr. Schneider had said, but I wondered if he'd said the same thing to everyone. "Peter Matterson, the flutist, Wilson Hendricks on clarinet and Joey Cameron, the pianist."

Peter and I were both seniors. I was going to Haverford to pursue a liberal arts education, but Peter had been accepted at the Curtis Conservatory in Philadelphia. He was a serious and talented musician who undoubtedly would have a successful musical career.

I was more concerned about Joey, the pianist, a ninth grader who'd been playing since he was five or six and whose parents were both musicians. He was probably the most gifted musician in the school and had Leonard Bernstein's ability to play any song from memory after hearing it once. I'd figured he'd easily win the competition, so the best I could do would be to come in second or third. Joey's main problem was his youthful overconfidence. I'd heard him play on other occasions where he'd been so intent on impressing his listeners that he'd rushed the notes and made careless mistakes.

My own problem was the opposite: a lack of confidence and nervousness. I'd considered playing the Honegger piece from memory but after a long night of tossing and turning had decided against it. This was, I decided, a musical competition rather than a memory contest.

Before the afternoon's events got underway, I was joined by my friend, Tony, whose job was to sit next to me and give me moral support. In addition to an extra copy of the music, he'd brought a large brown paper bag.

"I've noticed that when you're nervous, you tap your right toe to keep time," he said, and pulled a pair of black rubbers the size of my shoes out of the bag. "If you put these on, it will muffle the sound and not distract the judges from your playing."

It sounded totally ridiculous. No one had ever mentioned that before. Besides, it was a sunny day, and wearing rubbers would just make people laugh. We argued for a moment but he wouldn't give in.

"Okay," I said, finally. "Let's compromise. Since I usually tap with my right foot, I'll wear one rubber." I don't know if it made my toe-tapping any less conspicuous, but this little episode distracted me from my nervousness.

Before the competition began, the nine soloists drew lots to determine who would go first. I was next-to-last.

Peter, the flutist, went first, playing a slow and haunting Ravel composition. You could tell by the quality of his tone and breath control that he had been fortunate with good teachers who knew how to shape his innate talent.

"He's the one to beat," I whispered to Tony. He nodded in agreement.

The next four soloists followed in quick succession and didn't produce any memorable sounds. This gave my spirits a needed lift.

Then it was Wilson, the clarinetist's turn, who performed a beautiful transcription from a Bach sonata. It was a little over his head but it was nicely rendered and the audience gave Wilson an enthusiastic round of applause.

I leaned in again toward Tony. "Good God," I whispered. "Now there's two I've got to beat: Peter and this guy, Wilson." I was getting nervous again. Joey, the young, brash pianist was next. He sat down at the Steinway without any music in front of him. This dramatic gesture got everyone whispering. He waited until the audience fell silent and all eyes were fixed on him before beginning Beethoven's *Sonata in E flat major,* one of the most challenging of Beethoven's thirty piano sonatas.

He played it nearly flawlessly until the last movement. Then, as he reached the final crescendos, he suddenly stopped mid-passage. The room went silent. People looked at one another nervously and squirmed in their seats. I glanced at Tony. "Memory whiteout," he mouthed the words. A performer's worst nightmare. Then, suddenly, gorgeous sounds again flowed from the Steinway. The audience gave him a standing ovation. How could I compete with that? His midday brilliance against my nightlight in the bathroom.

When people had settled in their seats, the master of ceremonies stepped to the microphone. "Our next-to-last contestant is Lauro Halstead on trombone. He will be playing a selection from the *King David Oratorio* by the Swiss composer Arthur Honegger. He will be accompanied on the piano by Mr. William Schneider."

There was tepid applause as I stood before the audience with my music on the rack and the black rubber on my right shoe. I was terrified. Why had I let Bill Schneider pick one of the hardest pieces I had ever played? I looked over at my friend, Tony, who gave me a broad smile and a thumbs up sign. I took a deep breath and began to play.

I have no memory of what followed. I believe I played all the right notes and tried my best to make it sing even where there was no discernible melody. When I finished, there was a ripple of polite applause. I sat down as quickly as I could.

The last performer was the violinist, who played an excerpt from Vivaldi's *The Four Seasons*. It was a calm and reassuring performance which everyone enjoyed, but it was not a winner.

Of the nine soloists, my money was on Peter, the flutist. The head judge stepped to the microphone to announce the winners and the grand prize of $25. If the competition that day had been a contest for the best essay written in ancient Greek, the first prize money would have been $2000 or more. But this was 1953, and it would be many years before musical accomplishment at Andover would gain parity with more traditional, academic activities.

"The third prize and a check for $10 goes to Wilson Hendricks for his fine performance on the clarinet."

This left me feeling depressed. *If someone like that could get third place*, I figured to myself, *I was totally out of the running*.

"The second prize and a check for $15 goes

to Peter Matterson for his brilliant performance on the flute," the judge said. There was an enthusiastic burst of applause as Peter moved toward the front of the auditorium. *He deserved first place,* I thought.

"Finally, we come to the winner of today's competition," the judge said. "This was not an easy decision. Everyone should be proud of how he played today." He paused.

"I'm pleased to say," the judge continued, "it was a unanimous decision. The three of us agreed that today's winner of the annual Andover music competition is..." He held up the envelope with the $25 check and gave it a flourish. "The winner is," the judge winked at me as he glanced down at the rubber on my right shoe, "The winner is Lauro Halstead for his magnificent performance on the trombone."

*****

This was my one shining moment as a musician and a trombone player. I never entered another musical contest or dreamed of winning another competition. However, I didn't fall out of love with music. Far from it. I just didn't have the all-consuming passion needed to turn music into a professional career, to struggle and sacrifice for years and still be unable to get a job. My goal was to keep music as a mistress, and not make her my wife.

As it turned out, life events conspired to reinforce this decision. But that wouldn't happen for another year. After graduating from Andover, I spent a lazy summer doing odd jobs in my hometown and barely touched the trombone. I spent a few weeks taking piano lessons but didn't practice enough to make satisfying progress. I was at loose ends, and the piano wasn't going to tie them together.

When I arrived at Haverford in early September, I took my trombone with me, intending to resume playing. However, Haverford did not have a musical studies program, so everything I did was extracurricular. I played in the marching band and joined a jazz combo. I played in the Bryn Mawr-Haverford orchestra and at the end of the year was elected president. I also played briefly with a semi-professional chamber orchestra in the suburbs of Philadelphia.

The last concert I played in at the end of my freshman year was with the combined Bryn Mawr-Haverford orchestra and glee club which was supplemented with professional soloists. The program was Gabrielle Fauré's *Requiem Mass,* a magisterial piece of music whose melodies, especially the powerful, opening bars of the *Introit* and the sweet refrain of *Agnus Dei* still bring tears to my eyes. We played this glorious piece in early June, 1954, a week before I sailed to Europe. It was the last time I played the trombone and six weeks before I came down with poliomyelitis.

*****

Later that summer, as I lay in the respirator tank in Madrid, unable to breathe on my own due to polio, the memory of that last concert sustained and comforted me. I didn't view the Mass as morbid. To the contrary, it was life-enhancing, even lifesaving for this nonbeliever. To the rhythm of the respirator, I could endlessly replay in my mind my favorite passages from the mass all the way through to the final, soaring notes of *In Paradisium*. The music was so powerful that it made my heart beat stronger and made my breathing less labored. I could even think more clearly, and with more optimism. It was my private miracle. I could hear it any time I wanted, day or night, a few strains or a whole section at a time, right inside my own head.

A popular recording of the Requiem Mass.

And when my nurses—Catholic sisters whose divine task was to convert me before I expired—saw me smiling beatifically, these happy young virgins were convinced I was praying for mercy from their Jesus when, in fact, I was simply piping in my own salvation from another god. Did Fauré save my life? Possibly. Music can exert miraculous powers not only on listeners and performers but on a desperately ill teenager lying alone in an alien land.

Whether it was the prayers of the sisters or the miracle of the artificial respirator or the inspiration of Fauré's blessed music, or some combination of this holy trinity, I survived.

Yes, I survived! When I returned to college, people often asked if I grieved the loss of my ability to play music. Of course I did. However, that loss was inconsequential compared to my other losses: the use of my right arm, normal lung function, a healthy body image. These were losses that no amount of prayer or work could heal. Music, on the other hand, remained untouched in my soul. I could never play the trombone again, but I found other musical outlets.

While recovering in the rehabilitation hospital, I started playing piano with my left hand and when I returned to college I joined the men's glee club. When my children, Larissa, Christina and Alexander were young, I used to play simple tunes on an upright Yamaha piano to amuse them and to help them go to sleep at night. Larissa and Christina's favorite was the melancholy, traditional French song, *Plaisir d'Amour.*

"Play it again, Daddy," they'd call out from their beds. I'd play it again—six, eight, maybe ten times while they lay stretched out in the darkness struggling to stay awake.

The house fell silent; the soaring notes floated out upon the air; a wordless bond of love spread out and embraced us. Embraces us still.

The magic of music.

This was part of the enchantment of their

childhood and a priceless gift they bequeathed me. Playing the piano for my children led me to rediscover the forgotten pleasures of music in my life. By using the 'sustain' pedal on the piano, I could 'establish' chords with my left hand in the base and then, while those notes lingered in the air, swiftly move the fingers of my left hand to a higher register where I could improvise tunes that fit the chords. Sometimes with written music, and often without it, I played songs and harmonies that fit my mood for hours on end. Anything that pleased my ear and eased my soul.

My three beloved children: Larissa, Alexander and Christina.

Perhaps it was those childhood memories of

the magic of bedtime music that prompted all three children to study the piano. Eventually, for Christina and Larissa, practicing the piano gave way to acting, sports and school work. When Alex tired of the piano, he discovered a love and talent for playing the acoustic and electric guitars.

Playing the piano with one hand for my kids made me realize how much I missed making music in the company of other musicians during all the years that I hadn't played the trombone.

Then, late in 2007 I received a telephone call from an acquaintance from Andover, Lloyd Farrar, with whom I'd played trombone together in the dance band. After graduation, he'd gotten a degree in music and become a professional musician. We hadn't been close in school and I hadn't seen him since graduation more than 55 years earlier, but now he was trying to organize a reunion in June of old Andover dance band members to coincide with the annual school reunion.

"If we can get ten or twelve of the old guard together," Lloyd said, "We can do some jamming and put on a couple of concerts for old time's sake. It will be great fun."

He hadn't known about my polio and that I hadn't played trombone in over half a century.

"Don't worry about that," he said, after I told him my story. "I'm legally blind and still play all the time. If you can use your left hand, I can fix you up with a valve instrument like a baritone or euphonium." And so it happened. He was a representative of a brass instrument company in Eastern Europe and within several weeks, I owned a beautiful new euphonium built in the Czech Republic. I could still read music, but the more serious question concerned my lip which was 55 years out of shape. "Get yourself a teacher and give it time," Lloyd advised me. "Remember, to get your lip in shape, all it takes is practice."

Practice. I knew all about practice. Although Mr. DiSalvo was long gone, his one simple rule lived on in my heart. I quickly found a local master teacher, Dale Cheal, who guided me, step-by-step, in learning my new instrument. By the time I got to the musician reunion in June, I was able to hold my own and enjoy the camaraderie of classmates I hadn't seen in decades. And then it all came flooding back: all these sounds performed individually and then blending together to form gorgeous, pulsating harmonies. There is nothing comparable to playing with other musicians—all leaning in, intently focused, listening, mesmerized by the intoxicating rhythms and melodies. There were my notes and those of a trombone next to me, full and brassy; next to him were two tenor saxophones with a reedy, plaintive sound; behind me were the trumpets with their sharp, crisp runs; off to my left were a snare and bass drum and next to him a piano; on my far right two baritone saxes—low, full-throated, sexy. There were at least ten of us up on the stage of the main Andover auditorium, playing our hearts out to old favorites such as *Mood Indigo, Basin Street Blues* and *I'm in the Mood for Love.*

The beat was infectious. The audience clapped and even got up to dance in the aisles. The air filled with joy as old classmates smiled and giggled. It was easy to see the power of music, and how that power could create anything: love, forgiveness, or even a revolution. And now, once again, there I was among old friends, doing my part to spread love and happiness.

Practicing the euphonium at home.

The first songs were from our high school days. Then, as long as our lips held out, we played music from later eras throughout the weekend reunion: the Beatles, Fleetwood Mac, the Bee Gees, the Eagles. Late Saturday afternoon, a group of us who played brass instruments—myself on euphonium, Lloyd on trombone, three trumpeters and a French horn player—sneaked off to the Andover Chapel. This imposing structure featured a huge organ with a 32-foot bass pipe, the largest on the East Coast. That day we were permitted to sit in the cramped, high loft adjacent to the organist where our brass ensemble played classical pieces by Bach, Vivaldi, Handel and, at my request, Fauré, accompanied by the organ. It seemed we were playing up among the angels and the heavenly sounds filled the Chapel and spilled out onto the campus green.

Where had the years gone? How had I let music slip through my fingers? Suddenly, I was back in high school when I could still play my trombone, initially high in the chapel loft with the brass choir next to the organist, then up on the stage in the midst of the dance band, and, finally, in that small auditorium playing a selection from Honegger's *King David Oratorio* as a solo in the school's musical competition. Oh, how I'd missed music, especially creating music together with other dedicated musicians.

When I returned home, I joined several community bands hoping to replicate the pleasure I had experienced during the Andover reunion weekend. One group, *The Rockville Brass Band*, had outstanding musicians and a professional conductor. It was modeled after British brass bands, which are some of the best in the world. I played with them for several years until post-polio syndrome caused progressive weakness in my legs as well as new weakness in my left hand. I couldn't walk up the short hill from the parking lot to the rehearsal hall because of the pain in my legs; then the repeated flexing of my fingers to depress the valves on the euphonium caused my whole left hand to ache for days so, reluctantly, I resigned from this group.

However, I was still eager to play with some ensemble and so, together with another physician, we formed our own group which became known as *The District of Columbia Brass Quintet*. The great advantage of this group is that we rehearse in my home once a week and we play selections that don't overtax my fingers or embarrass our talent. It is a wonderful group of committed amateurs and the rehearsals give each of us an opportunity to express our joy and wonder in the magic of making music together.

Although my aging lip and painful hand don't allow it as much as before, I try to stay in shape, musically, as best I can. And there is still only one way forward: practice.

The District of Columbia Brass Quintet playing a concert in June 2014.

Family Matters

Chapter Thirteen: American Heroes

In June 1962, having just completed my third year of medical school, I received a travel grant to study tropical medicine in northern India for three months.

"I know you'll love the country," my mother said as we sat together in the *Air India* departure lounge at JFK airport waiting for my flight to board. "The food, the music, the hospitality. It's an ancient civilization with a lot to learn and enjoy."

She was something of an India expert. After graduating from college in 1928, she and my father had lived there for four years. Their lives, like those of millions of others, were changed and inspired by the great Mahatma Gandhi's fight for justice and Indian independence.

Through family connections, my father had been hired to be the dean of students at Lucknow Christian College in Uttar Pradesh state in northern India. It was not a job that he had trained for or one that suited his talents. He was simply a young white man looking for adventure in a brown man's world. As it turned out, he'd found plenty of it, as he and my mother got swept up in the cause of Indian freedom from British rule. Now, thirty years later, I was setting out for the same part of the world, seeking an adventure of my own.

I confessed to my mother that I was kind of nervous about the trip, having heard horror stories about India's heat, dangerous diseases, and heartbreaking poverty.

"Well, don't forget that we managed to survive," my mother said. "You'll do fine." My mother was in her mid-fifties and she still retained the youthful good looks and zest for life that had attracted my father. Now, sitting next to me in the airport, she took out an old black-and-white photograph of herself and my father taken before they left India in 1932.

My parents, Helen and Gordon, in India.
1930.

As Flight 212 for Rome and Bombay was called, my mother handed me the photograph as a keepsake for my trip. It captured the essence of their time in India: she was dressed in a sari and head scarf while he wore a drab Nehru jacket. She looked happy with her lips drawn back as though she were about to smile. I'd inherited her optimism that said 'yes' to the unknown and a wisdom that said, 'count your change.'

"Do you think anyone will remember what

you did back then?" I asked. My parents had been thrown out of India by the British for agitating for Indian independence.

"It's been thirty years," my mother replied. "And a lot has happened. We were just two young, idealistic Americans among millions who joined the fight." My mother glanced again at the photo. "It was a period of great political turmoil. Gandhi and Nehru were everywhere, organizing strikes and leading nonviolent demonstrations, especially on university campuses. I've never seen your father so excited about a cause."

My father was known in the family as a rabble-rouser, someone who tested limits and challenged authority. Although he considered himself a pacifist, in this photo he'd assumed a stiff, military-style pose perhaps to impress someone outside the frame. If my mother was the peacemaker, then he was the trouble-maker.

"Your father wanted India to be independent and wasn't content to just encourage the students. He wanted to be in the thick of things and do his part. He gave speeches and organized rallies. Here he was, a twenty-six-year-old American talking about liberty and freedom." My mother had told me this story many times before. "The students loved it," she added.

And my father loved it. So much so that he

thought he could single-handedly get the British to leave. Inspired by Martin Luther's challenge to papal authority, in late 1931 he wrote a manifesto addressed to the Viceroy, the top British official in India, with a list of demands that concluded, "India for Indians. Give them their independence."

The Viceroy's representative in Lucknow was not pleased. Who did Gordon Halstead think he was, telling the British Crown how to rule its empire? The representative called my father into his office, telling him to either withdraw his letter or leave the country within ten days. My parents loved India, and the idea of leaving it caused them great anguish. They argued back and forth for several days, but in the end decided to leave the country. My father wouldn't back down. Unexpectedly, his intransigence sparked widespread student demonstrations of support that lasted for over a week. For a brief period, they were national heroes.

Because of their influence, I had dreamed of visiting India for years, but now that I was about to board the plane, I suddenly wondered what I was getting into. Travel could be dangerous. Eight years earlier in 1954, I had barely survived a severe case of acute polio while hitchhiking in Europe.

"Final call," the gate attendant announced. "Gate 15, flight 212 for Rome and Bombay." I had to go.

"Only drink bottled water and eat in busy restaurants," my mother said as she gave me one last hug. It was the perfect advice for travelling to a developing country. Mother knew her stuff.

After landing in Bombay, I caught a train bound for Ludhiana, the largest city in Punjab state in the northwestern part of the country. My destination was the Christian Medical College, an institution known for its expertise in tropical medicine. For the next three months, I lived with Indian medical students in a simple dormitory; during the day I joined the other students at the teaching hospital where I participated in the evaluation and treatment of patients with common Third World diseases such as malaria, typhoid fever and cholera.

"Have you been upstairs to the isolation ward yet?" a fellow Indian student asked me one day after we'd finished patient rounds. "It's the scariest thing I've ever seen." It was hard to imagine anything worse than the death and suffering I had already seen. "They've got at least twenty patients up there and they're all dying from smallpox—little kids, old men, you name it. All covered with ugly sores and pustules."

I eventually got up the courage to visit this ward. As I opened the door, I was hit by the putrid stench of rotting flesh. But what I found most dispiriting was the absolute silence; no one talked and no one moved, not patients, not visitors, not even staff. It was as though death had already arrived. I decided on the spot that I wasn't tough enough for Third World medicine.

Everything I'd heard about India, both good and bad, was turning out to be true. My mother had been right to praise Indian hospitality. Virtually every weekend, I was invited to someone's home for dinner or a small party. Even hosts of modest means took great care to ensure that I was treated like visiting royalty. Through this network of friends, I received an invitation to a wedding celebration that joined two wealthy families and which turned out to be a festival as well as a feast. Chefs imported from New Delhi concocted up a banquet of exquisite delicacies served against a background of haunting, mystical sounds of eastern melodies played on traditional instruments. It was a magical, enchanted evening.

When there weren't afternoon teaching rounds at the hospital, I would join my medical school friends at the local theater to watch Bollywood films that portrayed classical tales of love and deceit with a level of refinement and artistry worthy of Oscar nominations. I was also impressed by how ordinary Indians, despite obvious hardships, maintained a sense of dignity and poise that reflected deep pride in a long and rich cultural heritage. It was easy for me to see why my parents had fallen in love with India so many years earlier.

However, there were other realities of Indian life that perhaps they'd forgotten. In late June, there were ten straight days of temperatures over 110°F; July was the beginning of monsoon season, and in early August there was an invasion of locusts so thick, the local paper reported, that motorists had to turn on their headlights. Although Ludhiana was a relatively prosperous city, overpopulation and signs of poverty were everywhere. In the early mornings while walking to the hospital, I passed little girls in rags with flat baskets who darted behind cows wandering in the streets to catch the manure before it hit the dusty pavement. Manure was a prized commodity that could be used for fertilizer, cooking and making bricks.

Beggars were everywhere, especially toddler girls, dressed to evoke feelings of pity and revulsion with birth defects and open wounds prominently displayed. At the local train station, I once saw two beggars—a tall, aristocratic-looking man who was blind and the other a young boy, no older than five or six, with no legs. To compensate for each other's disability and to beg as one, the aristocratic man who could not see carried on his shoulders the boy who could not walk. I was overwhelmed. I looked at my own useless right arm which suddenly seemed more like a trivial nuisance than a significant disability. After all, I could both see and walk.

"How can I be so self-centered?" I asked myself. I compared America and India: one flawed but arrogant in its abundant resources and youthful vigor; the other struggling but proud of its rich legacy and amazing resilience. I'm ashamed to say that I was too embarrassed by my own good fortune and ambivalence to give the beggars even a single rupee.

In addition to the patients I saw at the hospital, I joined a small group of students and their instructor each week as they made trips to rural areas to provide "Band-Aid" medicine at small, one-room clinics. The patients were mostly subsistence farmers who had given up on local shamans but were too poor to make the trip to the city. Often, this was their first encounter with a Western-style doctor, and their diseases tended to be serious.

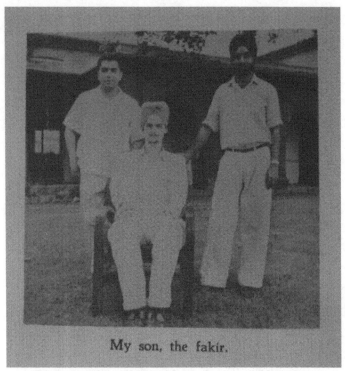

My son, the fakir.

Me (seated) with two Indian medical students. Ludhiana, India. July 1962.

One day, an elderly man with leprosy came to the clinic. His illness was so advanced that he'd lost all or part of each finger and several toes, his face was scarred and deformed and his nose totally eroded. I could understand why through the ages leprosy has caused such fear and prejudice. At a public swimming pool in Ludhiana, I'd seen a sign that read "No dogs or lepers allowed." Now, with this patient seated in front of me, just looking him in the eyes was difficult. *This is another human being,* I thought, as I tried not to look away. The encounter forced me to ask myself, *Where is my humanity?*

"People used to think that rats or other rodents chewed off the fingers," the instructor physician said, as we examined the patient together. Although I knew I couldn't become infected by just touching this man, the hairs on the back of my neck stood up in fear as I ran my fingers over his misshapen hand. I was ashamed of myself.

"The leprosy bacterium attacks the peripheral nerves so people can't feel their fingers," the instructor said. "Due to the loss of feeling, over time, repeated trauma to the fingertips causes the bones to slowly reabsorb and the fingers become smaller and smaller."

It was on one of these visits to a rural clinic that I was invited, along with the instructor, to have lunch in the home of the mayor of a nearby village. His house was a modest mud brick structure.

"Why did you come to India?" the mayor asked, while his wife poured tea. "You come from a rich country, and here we have so many problems with disease and poverty."

"I thought I might like to work in India one day," I replied. I didn't mention that I was in the process of changing my mind. "My parents used to live here a long time ago. They loved it and I guess I always wanted to follow in their footsteps." I described my parents' experience in India thirty years earlier when they were expelled for their support of independence and hailed by university students as heroes. He seemed quite interested in what I was saying. "May I be knowing the names of your parents, please?" he asked.

"Halstead," I replied. "Gordon and Helen Halstead." He thought for a moment and then got up and left the room. He returned a short while later, smiling.

"I think this might be your parents, isn't it?" He held in his hand a postcard with a grainy picture of a young Western couple dressed in Indian clothes. I was dumbfounded. Yes, it was Helen and Gordon all right.

"Those are my parents!" I exclaimed. "How in the world do you have their picture in your house?"

"I was a university student in Calcutta," he said. "Your father was well known for his activities on behalf of independence. He even visited our campus several times. When the British asked him to leave, we students went on strike to protest."

My host closed his eyes as though recalling a memory. "On their way back to America, your parents' train stopped in Calcutta. I went with several of my friends to wave goodbye and show our support. I bought this postcard as a souvenir." He opened his eyes and with great emotion said, "Please tell your parents we still remember them. It was our struggle but they stood shoulder-to-shoulder with us. They are true American heroes."

Chapter Fourteen:
Blessings from My Father

"What's happening to me?" I asked Richard, a psychologist friend from the hospital where I'd been working in Houston for the past two years.

"What do you mean?" Richard said. It was a warm, spring afternoon, and we'd just seen a Saturday matinee together. The film was a romantic comedy; not at all sad. But emerging from the dark movie theater into the bright afternoon sunlight, I was wiping tears from eyes.

"I don't know," I said. "I don't cry easily. But toward the end of the movie, out of the blue, I felt tears streaming down my cheeks."

"Has this ever happened before?"

"Not that I remember."

Richard's tone became professional. "Was there something in the movie, you know, a character, an emotion, dialogue that struck some kind of nerve?"

I suddenly felt like his patient. But I couldn't think of anything. "No, I enjoyed the movie. I'm a little tired after a long week but I wasn't feeling particularly sad."

We went into a nearby restaurant for a late lunch. By the time we got to dessert, I'd completely forgotten about crying, but Richard hadn't. "That thing with your tears," he said.

He took a sip of coffee and looked into my eyes. "I don't think you should ignore it."

I smiled, hoping to deflect his serious expression.

"I know you'll deny it," he said. "But I wonder if there isn't some underlying sadness. Something that's been covered over for years that you're not even remotely aware of."

Preposterous, I said. I was the youngest of three children, who'd had adoring parents and a happy childhood. I added that my wife was pregnant with our first child. I'd finally found a job I thoroughly enjoyed. No, I didn't feel the least bit sad. To the contrary, I felt fortunate. So why didn't he just bugger off and go analyze someone who had real problems.

Fortunately, my friend Richard didn't just "bugger off" and forget about it. Instead, a few days later at the hospital, he invited me to join him for coffee.

"I've been thinking some more about your unexpected tears," he said. "I don't think it's anything serious, but it would probably be worthwhile to talk with someone for a couple of sessions."

Either he caught me by surprise or my defenses had been weakening since we had seen the movie together. I decided to hear him out.

"No big deal," he assured me. "But if you're willing to see someone, here's the name of a psychologist I'd recommend." He handed me a piece of paper with a name and telephone number.

"Tell him I suggested you call," he said. "I'm confident you'll like him."

I did like Dr. Eric Rogers. However, instead of meeting me one-on-one as I'd expected, he put me in a small group of men and women who were all about my age and dealing with a variety of issues.

During the first session, I felt too shy to say anything more than my name. Then, during the second session, a woman sitting next to Dr. Rogers looked over at me. "Lauro, I'm sure we'd all like to hear what you have to say," she said. "Why did you join our group?"

It was a straightforward question, asked with genuine interest. Yet I felt on the spot. I glanced around the room. Everyone was looking at me. But I told myself they weren't there to grill me. No, everyone was there seeking help, looking for support, trusting that others were there to embrace them. I took a deep breath and tried to steady my nerves. Dr. Rogers smiled at me. And then I realized that everyone in the group was smiling at me, eager to hear what I had to say. These were people who wished me well. These were people who, without knowing anything about me but my name, were reaching out to me in a caring way.

It was too much.

Tears started streaming down my cheeks. I

was crying, then sobbing and then, overcome with emotion, I stopped breathing for a moment.

When I finally regained my composure, I described crying at the movies. To my surprise, a similar thing had happened to several other members of the group. In the case of a middle-aged man named Marvin, it was because he had lost a sibling when they were both quite young. He had suppressed his grief and was totally unaware of his deep sadness until one day, all at once, he'd started crying. Another member of the group, Elizabeth, a recent divorcee, had unaccountably begun crying when she was out on a date with a new boyfriend. Her sadness stemmed from her childhood relationship with an unaffectionate mother.

Her story got us talking about our parents and the amount of affection they'd shown us as we were growing up. When it was my turn, I had to admit that while my mother was demonstrative, there had not been a lot of emotional displays of affection in our home. Yes, I'd known I was loved; my mother, Helen, had told me that repeatedly.

My father, Gordon, on the other hand, was much more reserved. But I knew that, in his quiet way, he loved me. How did I know? Well, I just did. Except for occasional outbursts of anger, Gordon was not a man who showed emotion easily and he certainly didn't run around shouting "I love you," even to his son. But I'd always thought that my father kept his emotions in check because he cared so much. Still waters ran deep, after all. I was sure his love for me was very deep, indeed.

"When's the last time one of your parents hugged you?" Dr. Rogers asked.

"My mother hugs me all the time," I said.

"How about your father?"

"Um..." I considered the question. But Dr. Rogers already knew the answer.

"Can you remember *any* time when your father hugged you?" he asked. I tried to think back: this year, last year, during my childhood.

"I'm sure...maybe..." I couldn't finish the sentence.

"When's the last time he said he loved you?" Marvin asked.

That did it.

I started crying again and then, one by one, the people in the group came over to give me a hug. I knew Gordon loved me. He was simply not a man who showed emotion easily.

"When's the next time you're going to see your father?" Elizabeth asked. My parents were retired and living in an old farmhouse in southern Vermont. I tried to visit every time I went back East, maybe three or four times a year. I was scheduled for a visit in a month, toward the end of May.

"Would you be willing to write him?" someone asked. "Tell him you're coming home and *you* want to give *him* a hug. Don't wait for him. You take the lead."

In American culture, we've long considered the father to be the family provider, the one who leaves the home daily to work and bring home the bacon. Focusing on earning a salary and advancing in the workforce, American men inevitably have less time and energy to devote to their roles as husbands and fathers. Unfortunately for many families, however, a vicious cycle is often set in motion whereby men achieve more gratification from outside activities (work, clubs, sports) than they do at home. One of the saddest results is the lost opportunity for that special kind of love that occurs with genuine father-son bonding: the son is deprived of the wisdom and nurturing that only a father can offer. As he grows up, the son also seeks to become a provider, and so leaves his home for school, work, and eventually, his own family. Sometimes living far from his family of origin, the son retains memories of promises unfulfilled. Age mocks what might have been.

Writing to my father turned out to be good advice. I wrote and told him about the group, my new insights and my plan to hug him during my next trip home. To my surprise, he wrote back almost immediately. He apologized for not being more expressive and promised to

make up for it in the future. He said that showing emotion among men born in the Victorian
era was not easy. Born in 1905, he'd come from
Dutch-English stock that was famous for main-
taining a stiff upper lip.

My father had had the added disadvantage
of not having a father at home to serve as a role
model during his own childhood. My mother
had told me that my Dad's father had abandoned the family when Dad was only two, and
he had seen his own father maybe a dozen
times in his whole life. This was a story that
could bring tears to anyone's eyes.

When I flew home in late May, my parents
met me at the small regional airport. They were
already on the tarmac, standing by a gate in the
chain-link fence as I was getting off the plane.
The moment I passed through the gate, my father stepped toward me with his arms
stretched out wide.

"Lauro, my adorable son," he said as he gave
me a bear hug. "I love you. I love you. Welcome
home." Both of us were crying. I was overcome
with emotion.

"Dad, I love you," I said. "I've always loved
you. I'm so glad you're still alive so I can tell
you that."

My mother was beside herself with joy. I
embraced her and then told her how much—
how very much—I loved her. It was a marvel-

ous visit home. However, the hugs at the airport were not the high point.

Dr. Rogers had suggested that I take my parents out to a nice restaurant, but one at a time. "The dynamic changes completely when it's one-on-one instead of two-on-one," he said.

It was great advice. My father and I had never gone out to a restaurant by ourselves, just the two of us. I'd always gone out with both parents.

This dinner alone with him resulted in the longest conversation we had ever had. It was the first time we'd talked, really talked, adult to adult, soon-to-be-father to father.

"Tell me about your father," I said.

"I didn't know him at all, really," he said. There was a long pause while he wiped tears from his eyes. "He ran off with another woman before I was two. When he finally stopped by the house a few years later, I thought he was a stranger off the streets."

He then told me he hadn't seen his father more than twenty times in his whole life, even though he'd grown up in White Plains, New York, a city less than thirty miles from Manhattan, where his father lived.

"When I was in college," Dad continued, "I wrote to my father for some money to help with college expenses. He wrote back saying he was sorry but he didn't have any extra money. It was only one of two letters he ever wrote me."

I couldn't conceive of the sadness, unhappiness and injury this abandonment must have caused my father. How does a child cope with a parent he has never known? I forgave Dad on the spot that evening for being emotionally remote.

For a while we made idle chatter about the tasty food at the restaurant and retired life in southern Vermont. I told him about Houston and how much I enjoyed living in the Southwest. This got us talking about my new job at the rehabilitation hospital and how I thought I had finally found a niche in medicine where I could feel fulfilled.

"I'm really proud of you," he said, "proud of what you have accomplished and proud of what you have overcome in life." When he said that, I assumed he was referring to my becoming a physician despite my disability. Or, perhaps, my struggles to discover a satisfying career path. I was grateful for his praise.

However, I soon realized he was talking about something much more profound. He was comparing what I was doing with my life with what he had done with his.

How could he make such a comparison?

Here was a man who had grown up without a father in the home; a man who had gone off to India right out of college and had stood up to the British Empire for Indian independence; a man who had been a whistleblower in job after job only to lose each job for his principles; a man who had helped raise three successful children; a man who'd preached socialism but in the middle of the Depression, had exhausted the family's savings to buy a treasure of a farmhouse in Vermont on a whim; a man who did precinct politics all his life and then at the age of 87 ran for a seat in the Vermont Legislature; a man who had been home for dinner on time, helped with the dishes and had shown up at all my music recitals and graduations.

And what had I done, for Christ's sake? I'd done my homework, survived a serious illness, studied hard, obtained a graduate degree and then a divorce. There was no confronting the British Empire or whistleblowing for me. I'd kept my head down and stayed in line. What kind of comparison was that? And yet, toward the end of dinner, just before the check arrived, my father leaned in so close our heads were almost touching.

"You have no idea how proud I am of you," he said. Then he said the words I'll never forget: "You are ten times the man I am."

Ten times? Twenty times? One hundred times? Who cared what the multiple was? It was meaningless. He was my father. He had been dealt a difficult hand. What was unfortunate, even tragic, was the fact that he saw himself as a failure, and not as the great man he was and remains in my memory.

On the way home in the car that night, I told him exactly how great I thought he was. "You have done important things in your life and I brag about you to my friends all the time. But the single most important thing you have done is to be my father."

My words were a great comfort to him—better, perhaps, than years of therapy. We had breached a wall that evening, and, in the years that followed, there was an openness in our conversations that had never existed before. As important as our deepening relationship was to me, I believe it was equally important to him. And I believe the new honesty that we shared contributed in some small way to the peace and serenity he experienced in his twilight years.

There was one other legacy from this visit with my father. When I finally had my children, two girls and a boy, I made sure that I hugged them daily and told them frequently how much I loved them. I didn't want any of them leaving a movie theater crying unexpectedly.

My parents, Helen and Gordon, in their golden years.

Afterword

When I set out to tell my story in the preceding pages, I wanted to describe a number of important events that shaped my life and gave it meaning. But, as I progressed, I realized there were many things people wondered about that didn't fit neatly into one chapter or another. So I decided to include a few of these thoughts in this Afterword.

*****

After reviewing an early draft of the manuscript, a colleague with whom I used to work at the MedStar National Rehabilitation Hospital in Washington, D.C. asked me, "Didn't your illness overwhelm you with depression and make you want to give up on life?"

This is how I tried to answer her: When I was stricken, I knew I was very sick, but it was impossible for me to see the larger picture. With no prior experience of paralysis, there was no way I could imagine what a lifetime of disability would be like, especially at the age of eighteen. Also, I was simply much too sick to process what was happening to me. Once my fever abated, I started to feel better and I experienced the first glimmer of hope—the real beginning of my recovery. When my mother finally arrived in Spain, we established some goals together. She was always inclined to look on the bright side of things, which really lifted my spirits. Early on, our goals were modest—they included my spending more time each day off the respirator, straightening out one of my legs by myself, or holding my breath to a count of three. Later, our milestones would grow more ambitious.

I inherited my mother's natural optimism, and my positive attitude was strongly reinforced by a series of events when I returned to the United States. The polio epidemics of the early 1950's had galvanized both the fear and sympathy of the American people, who treated polio survivors like minor celebrities. On my admission to the rehabilitation center near our home in White Plains, New York, two of my first visitors were a newspaper reporter and photographer. The following day, my picture was on the front page of the local newspaper, along with a long article describing my courageous fight to regain my health. There was no mention of my residual paralysis.

This attention was not unique to my case, but was characteristic of the national response to the polio epidemics. The sense that the community at large really cared was reinforced by the March of Dimes, which organized the door-to-door Mothers' Marches to collect funds for the recovery of polio survivors, including myself. All of this contributed to a sense of hope and optimism, along with the subtler message we polio survivors received: *Don't let America down by not getting well.* And as I did get stronger, everybody—my family, my friends, and the community—remained at my side to encourage me on to as complete a recovery as possible. It all seemed a part of the national mood and the can-do American spirit so prevalent in the postwar years. With so much going for me, how could I let my country down with a selfish case of depression?

*****

A number of years ago, when I helped run a program in Human Sexuality in Houston, I'd get this question all the time: "Can polio patients have a normal sex life?"

I used to dodge this a little by talking about *all* polio patients. More recently, I've felt more comfortable making it a first person narrative. I don't believe I worried about this issue while still fighting to breath in the wooden respirator. I was much more focused on emptying my bladder and having regular bowel movements—not being able to do so caused great discomfort. Which, oddly, showed me that my inner sensations were fully preserved. Lying on my back or side in one position for several hours made my skin burn and itch, which let me know that external sensation was also fully normal.

With my thoughts distracted by how well individual organs were functioning, I didn't spend much time worrying about whether I was still attractive to members of the opposite sex. In high school and my first year of college, I'd hardly dated, and had never had a steady girlfriend. Like most American teenagers, I thought about sex constantly, but it was a foreign land that I had never visited. It didn't help that I was shy and self-conscious in the presence of girls.

This changed dramatically and unexpectedly during my stay in the rehabilitation center, where I was assigned to a young, attractive and deliciously curvy physical therapist. Most of the therapy sessions were done behind screens or curtains so there was a fair amount of privacy. One day, I hardly knew what to do when she encouraged me, as part of an exercise, to lean back against her chest. I landed squarely against her soft breasts, which she seemed to enjoy as much as I. It was a divine feeling that we repeated frequently in subsequent days. However, even better things were in store.

After several months, it was clear that we were both infatuated. I was a tall, blond, eighteen-year-old world traveler whom adversity had hardened and matured. In addition, I was a graduate of a prestigious prep school and had been elected outstanding freshman at one of the best liberal arts colleges in the country. Altogether, a good catch. She was the charming and hard-working daughter of immigrants who was advancing in her profession. And it was clear that she didn't just feel sorry for me—she really liked me. She was a girl who could have had anyone, and she chose me. No—she didn't just *choose* me, she *wanted* me. And with that gorgeous body.

After I was released from rehab and had returned to college, she invited me to her house one day during spring break for an afternoon of studying. It was a perfect setup for fireworks. But we were both very much children of the 1950's—this was an age when a Hollywood movie in Times Square was boycotted because it contained the word "virgin." We both wanted sex, but were too shy to ask—at least, I was. At one point she left the room where we were studying; a short time later, she called me to join her in her bedroom. I found her stretched out on her bed, completely naked. A flawless body with a Florida tan. I'd never seen such beauty, much less been invited to lie down in its presence. But as much as we both wanted to be joined together that day, the fear of pregnancy hung like a heavy moral sword over the two of us. Crazy as it sounds, we were both content to settle for a simple, passionate kiss. We couldn't have been any better behaved if her mother was hiding in the closet.

Even in the absence of consummation, the experience was the best possible medicine—and one that I wish every youthful disabled person might enjoy. My right arm may have been paralyzed and my trunk frail from atrophy and weight loss, but I was attractive to this gorgeous woman, and my sexuality was not the least impaired. It was a glorious sensation and a precious piece of knowledge that, despite my innate shyness, would allow me, in the years ahead, to fulfill my desires as a man.

*****

"How is your life now?" a psychologist I have known for some time recently asked me. "What are the joys and sorrows as you approach your 80th year?"

It's a reasonable question. The past three to five years have been the hardest of my life—even more difficult than the early days of my recovery in the summer of 1954. Then, I had a tank full of youthful energy and optimism, as well as ignorance of what lay ahead. The world was pulling for me to fulfill my early promise, and the future sparkled with possibilities.

Now that tank is almost empty and there is

less sparkle up ahead. But this doesn't strike me as either unusual or depressing. Who can complain when one is allotted eight decades of continuous challenges and adventure? As for fulfilling that early promise, I will let others be the judge of that. What I know to be true is that I did my best to persevere and have no regrets about declining the priest's offer of last rites years ago in Madrid.

What has made the past few years especially difficult is the gradual loss of strength, primarily in my legs but more recently in my trunk and good left arm. This has been accompanied by pain—confined, for now, to failing muscles. Pain and weakness, an odd couple that comes calling in old age: pain perverts the want while weakness degrades the doing.

Travel is especially difficult. Every trip out of the house requires meticulous planning. One might say that I beat polio the first time around. From respirator to medical school and beyond was quite a leap. The second time around, post-polio syndrome is a very different story. There will be no miraculous restoration of function. There will be no reversal of my private, progressive weakness that has stretched out over the past thirty-five years. Youth was spent long ago—as it should be— and there simply are no more leaps.

The amazing recovery of strength that allowed me not just to walk, but to climb to the summit of Mount Fuji, was based on some well-established facts of anatomy and pathology. The first thing to understand is that the polio virus kills nerves, *not* muscles, which is counterintuitive since the patient experiences muscle paralysis. The common assumption is that the virus attacks the muscles directly. Instead, the viral attack aims at the nerves that stimulate the muscles to contract. When these nerves are killed, the corresponding muscles are robbed of their stimulation and become weak or paralyzed. Physicians call these muscles "orphaned," because they have lost the nerves that gave them life and made them contract.

What we now know is that over a period of several months or years, the remaining healthy nerves unaffected by the virus slowly reach out to "rescue" and stimulate the orphaned muscles, allowing them to contract and regain lost strength.

What I experienced was fairly typical of polio survivors but no less miraculous. The virus killed nerves all over my body, but especially in my legs. For the first few weeks, I was almost completely paralyzed. Then, little by little, over the subsequent weeks and months, as the remaining healthy nerves reached out to the "orphaned" paralyzed muscles, my strength returned. At first, I could move my legs more freely over my sheets. Then, I was strong enough to sit on the edge of my bed and "pump" my legs in the air. Eventually, I was allowed to get into a therapeutic swimming pool and, with the water supporting much of my weight, I was able to "walk" for the first time. After two or three months, with the healthy nerves stimulating more and more of my muscle fibers, I had enough strength to take a few steps on dry land. When I was finally discharged from the rehabilitation hospital in early January 1955, five months after the initial attack, I was not only walking unassisted but starting to climb stairs. By the end of the month, I was able to return to college as a part-time student.

There is, however, a downside to this extraordinary recovery of strength. For many polio survivors, the so-called "rescue nerves" work overtime for decades, at which point they begin to degenerate and die off, a process that leads to the onset of new muscle weakness or post-polio syndrome (PPS). For these individuals, there are no more rescue nerves available. There is no magical recovery of strength and function.

In my case, PPS began in 1982 or 83, when I was nearing fifty, approximately thirty years after my acute illness. During those three decades, I had walked and climbed stairs as much as I liked, as no one knew the wisdom of moderation. My rescue nerves were vastly over-worked and exhausted. When my muscles began to weaken, there were no fresh rescue nerves available to come to their aid.

This is the story of PPS. It doesn't kill, but it does slowly rob you of your strength and independence. And this is where I am today. I need help getting dressed in the morning and I use wheeled mobility wherever I go. This past year I started using a motorized wheelchair in the house and began using a hospital bed so that I can get in and out on my own. I sit on a raised toilet seat and use a voice activated dictation system rather than type with my fingers. I try to conserve my hand strength for practicing and playing the euphonium in the brass quintet, still a major source of joy.

Friends often want to know if I am discouraged or depressed. The answer is an emphatic *no*. Somehow, my optimism survives and I take great pleasure in the many joys that come my way each day. My wife, Jessica, forms the indispensable inner circle of love and support that helps me thrive. She is a medical anthropologist with a specialty in disability. A perfect partner if you happen to be disabled. We have been married for twenty-four years and she has, with grace and patience, made the necessary adjustments in her life to keep me productive at work and at home as my independence and strength have slowly ebbed away.

Our son, Alexander, who is pursuing his passion for film and video, is on the brink of graduating from college and launching a productive career. He has only known me as a disabled father, and has accepted my limitations as easily as he has accepted my height and the color of my eyes.

Just beyond these two, there is another circle of love and caring that contains my former wife of nineteen years, Kris, and the two daughters we raised together: Larissa, a highly skilled social worker who is married to Craig Royal and together they are the parents of the enchanting toddler Brooklyn Grace; and Christina, who recently completed her training as a social worker and looks forward to an adventurous future full of promise. They love me for my spirit and sense of humor and are totally at ease about the braces on my legs and the wheelchair they help me push from time to time. Fortunately, these two circles of people I love and cherish overlap easily and frequently, which enriches all of our lives.

Finally, there is the great pleasure I have had in reading, writing and conversing in Italian, and for the past eight years, in playing the music I love in an ensemble. More recently, now that I am retired, I have discovered the joy of writing this memoir, though it barely leaves time for the political gossip that is one of the obligations of living in the nation's capital.

My daughters, Christina and Larissa, with my mother, Helen, at age 101.

My granddaughter, Brooklyn Grace Royal.

*****

Over the years I have been repeatedly asked a question that might be better answered by a philosopher: Was getting polio a blessing? This question always makes me angry. No, polio was not a blessing. Rather, it was, and is, a curse. Life can be hard enough without the burden of a disability, no matter how mild. And polio, for me, has not been a single, fixed impairment you could adjust to, like a 20-pound stone I could expect to always carry around.

No, it was a stone that kept changing weight.

When I regained my health and my legs were feeling strong, the stone barely weighed a single pound and I hardly noticed it. As I climbed Mount Fuji, the stone felt as if it weighed forty pounds. These days, now that I am older, and my legs have become permanently weaker, I feel loaded down with at least fifty pounds. Others my age who are in good health carry no such stones.

What makes polio a special burden for many of us is that this disease of our youth, described in textbooks as static, keeps changing. I adjust to new weakness with another brace or scooter, but the weakness doesn't take notice, and soon I need to make yet another adjustment with a more powerful scooter or a longer brace. Aging doubtless plays a role, but is it fair to add to the struggles of aging a chronic disease that doesn't stop changing? It's enough to wear out my positive feelings about the universe.

Did polio in some perverse way enrich my life? I suppose that's possible. I may not have become a physician, and instead might have lived a carefree life in southern France making my own wine and perfecting my use of irregular verbs. As it is, being a disabled adult has given me a perspective on life I wouldn't otherwise have had, and this was especially useful while working with adults who were truly, profoundly disabled with spinal cord injuries. I can't say that I knew what it was like to have a spinal injury, but my empathy for those young people was real, which enhanced my role as a healer. And it definitely gave me a strong incentive to research ways to ease their suffering. As for polio survivors and the late effects of polio, I don't believe I would have explored this area if I hadn't had polio myself. Studying one's own disease as a physician provides a shortcut to becoming an expert. Being one of the first to identify post-polio syndrome was the crowning achievement of a medical career that, ironically, bent the personal arc of my own illness full circle.

So, yes. These experiences *have* enriched my life beyond measure. However, on balance, I can honestly say polio has been both a curse and a blessing. But what well-lived life doesn't contain a little of both?

36044960R00154

Made in the USA
San Bernardino, CA
13 July 2016